GOD,
CREATION,
and ALL THAT
JAZZ

GOD, CREATION,

and ALL THAT

JAZZ

A Process *of* Composition *and* Improvisation

ANN PEDERSON

Chalice Press®

St. Louis, Missouri

Cover and interior design: Elizabeth Wright
Art direction: Elizabeth Wright

This book is printed on acid-free, recycled paper.

Visit Chalice Press on the World Wide Web at
www.chalicepress.com

10 9 8 7 6 5 4 3 2 1   01 02 03 04 05 06

Library of Congress Cataloging–in–Publication Data

Pederson, Ann.
    God, creation, and all that jazz : a process of composition and improvisation /
by Ann Pederson.
        p.   cm.
    Includes bibliographical references.
    ISBN 0-8272-1246-1
    1. Creation.   I. Title.
BT695   .P43   2001
230' .046 − dc21   00-010286

Printed in the United States of America

CONTENTS

PREFACE

The idea for this project began almost six years ago over a pot of tea in Oxford, England, with the Reverend Dr. Arthur Peacocke. On this first trip to England, I sat down and talked with Arthur Peacocke about my interests in religion and science. I had only been involved in the actual dialogue between the two for about four years. Although we started out talking about religion and science, we soon found ourselves sharing our mutual love of music and the arts. We were both pianists; we both loved Bach. After leaving the Peacocke residence, I walked down to the famous Blackwell's Bookstore and purchased a copy of recent book Peacock's *Theology for a Scientific Age*. Unlike many theological texts, I read it with the same enthusiasm with which I read a novel. I discovered that Peacocke brought together his love of music with religion and science by offering the image of God as composer. Not only does Peacocke propose the model of God as composer, he also suggests that the improvisational arts of jazz and the blues might be the modern musical idiom for expanding on a classical model of God and the world. His suggestion stayed with me, and from that I have been developing the model of improvisation for imagining the relationship between God and the world. To Arthur Peacocke I owe not only professional acknowledgment of his work but also great appreciation for his friendship and mentoring.

In my own Lutheran tradition, music has always been the language of expressing the Christian faith. From the great chorales of Johann Sebastian Bach to the organ improvisations by Paul Manz, music often expresses the power of the gospel in ways that preaching and teaching do not, I believe. Music reaches down deep and breaks open our cognitive frameworks. We "think" in new ways through the power of music. Rationality is wrapped and embodied in the interactive process of the aesthetic and emotive power of music. In the short story "Sonny's Blues" (which I discuss in chapter 4), James Baldwin writes about the power of music:

> All I know about music is that not many people ever really hear it. And even then, on the rare occasions when something opens within, and the music enters, what we mainly hear, or hear corroborated, are personal, private, vanishing evocations. But the man who creates the music is hearing something else, is dealing with the roar rising from the void and imposing order on it as it hits the air. What is evoked in him, then, is of another order, more terrible because it has no words, and triumphant, too, for that same reason. And his triumph, when he triumphs, is ours.[1]

The triumph of music lies in its power to create, to impose order on chaos. Music creates and transforms the emptiness into creation, the chaos into order. The creativity of the musical composition is not the sole possession of the composer but a joint process among the composer, those who play the music, and those who listen. Music is a participatory process by which creativity occurs.

The opening movement of the Christian faith is expressed through the music of God's grace. Creation is the composition of God's grace. How does God compose this world in which we live? Like the maestro with the score written from all eternity? Or like the composer/conductor of a jazz ensemble? The primary model of composition, like the themes of classical theism, has been that of a classical orchestra conductor. I join a growing chorus of voices, from feminist theologians to those in religion and science, who find this classical model unhelpful for two reasons: (1) It does not resonate with the world described by the sciences, and (2) it does not fit with the strategies we need to traverse the boundaries of a messy, ambiguous, and pluralistic world. Although I do not want to simply jettison the themes of past generations, I believe that we are called to improvise on them in ways that can be heard anew. The traditional models of God and the world, while still helpful as themes on which to build, do not adequately convey the creative presence of God's action in the world. Neither do they provide a helpful strategy for helping Christians address the issues in our complex, messy world. The model of improvisation, particularly in jazz and the blues, can help us deepen and expand our insights into the creative process of God's composition. Therefore, I have chosen the model of improvisation for re-visioning the relationship between God and the world, and for developing a strategy Christians can use to live and be faithful to God's word in this world we call creation.

The themes of improvisation fit with my theological roots in feminist and process thought. The model of jazz emphasizes cooperative and creative relationships, empowers the individual while preserving the community, and adapts to novelty while conserving tradition. Jazz has always developed within a diverse musical community using a diversity of players. The players become internally related to the composition and the composer itself. Feminist theologians remind me of the musicians in the jazz ensemble; that is, they improvise on theological themes to create new compositions. Like the music in jazz, feminist theology recovers unheard voices, plays with their words and ideas, and composes them into new but familiar compositions. The ensemble is always diverse, adapting to the context of the current players while remaining attentive to the voices of past traditions. Feminist theologians are among many of the current improvisers on the Christian tradition—creating new compositions, recovering forgotten voices, and working together in diverse communities.

Part of my hope for this book is to help people think creatively about their faith and the world in which we live. This goal will be accomplished if people feel free to take this model and use it for further provocation, reflection, and action. I have taken materials from tradition and recombined them in ways that I hope are both faithful to tradition and applicable to our lives. Like the nature of improvisation itself, the theology presented in this book is meant to be used for further improvisation and reformation of tradition. Coming from a Lutheran background, I hope that the church is always in the process of reforming (*ecclesia semper reformanda*). I know from experience in my own theological tradition what happens when the church stops reforming. The gospel fits neither Word nor world.

The structure of this book functions somewhat like the performance of a jazz composition: Each chapter begins with a theme (the head); the themes are played and improvised; and the theme is restated at the end (repetition of the head). The purpose of this book is not to provide a traditional systematic approach to the doctrine of creation, but to create a composition where a variety of voices and themes are played together for the reader's own creative interpretation. The final product is created by the text, the reader's ideas and interactions, and the larger community's contextual boundaries. The argument of the book is constructed in the following way:

Chapter 1: The Composition of Creation. *How we perceive the composition of creation is essential to our understanding of God's relationship to the world and the meaning and purpose of human existence.*

Chapter 2: Creativity as Creaturely Vocation. *Creativity is God's gracious gift to humankind to be used in shaping and improvising with the creation for the purpose of transforming the world and living a fuller, more meaningful life.*

Chapter 3: Perfecting the Art of "Hanging Out." *We become who we are through the relationships we develop over time.*

Chapter 4: The Blues: An Affirmation That Life Still Swings. *In the music of the blues, I hear voices that know the depths of suffering and evil, but confront that evil with resistance and grace.*

Chapter 5: The Life of the Church. *The church's mission is to improvise on the theme of God's creative love and grace in each generation.*

In each chapter, I try to create a conversation of sorts among my personal reflections, themes from the Christian tradition, and current voices from feminism, process thought, and the religion and science dialogue. I was labeled a "wanton eclectic" by a Lutheran friend who had also been given that title. The plurality of voices in this book reflects my own interests and theological musings. For some people the plurality will sound like a cacophony; for others my hope is that the diversity will provide new ways to listen to the music of God's grace.

As I mentioned before, I owe the initial idea for this project to Arthur Peacocke. My thanks and appreciation for his work in the religion and science dialogue run deep. I am also deeply indebted to the theological work of Philip Hefner and Paul Sponheim, two of my Lutheran mentors. I see their creative work as continuous improvisation on not only the Lutheran tradition but also, and most importantly, on the Christian faith's relevance to the world.

Other voices have contributed greatly to the production of this book. Through the entire process, several persons have read the manuscript and offered helpful comments: Nancy Dickinson, Ann Grauvogl, Patrick Henry, Doris Milliken, Paul Sponheim, Lisa Stenmark, and Annelise Strommen. To my husband, Gary, I am deeply indebted for his knowledge of music, but most important, for his continual spiritual and moral support to complete this project. Finally, I would like to dedicate this book to Charles W. Milliken (my father) and Vernon C. Holmquist (my uncle), who constantly reminded me from an early age that jazz was the music that really mattered. To them, I owe this spiritual and musical ancestry.

1

THE COMPOSITION OF CREATION

For many years I have been interested in the arts of
improvisation, which involve recombining partly familiar
materials in new ways, often in ways especially sensitive to
context, interaction, and response...Jazz exemplifies artistic
activity that is at once individual and communal,
performance that is both repetitive and innovative, each
participant sometimes providing background support and
sometimes flying free.

Just as change stimulates us to look for more
abstract constancies, so the individual effort to compose a
life, framed by birth and death and carefully pieced
together from disparate elements, becomes a statement on
the unity of living. These works of art, still incomplete, are
parables in process, the living metaphors with which we
describe the world.

MARY CATHERINE BATESON[1]

HOW WE perceive the composition of creation is
essential to our understanding God's relationship to the world
and the meaning and purpose of human existence. In a world

*where there isn't one universal voice, or one song, the image of
improvisation in jazz and the blues offers an alternative way of
creating and playing with the composition of God's creation.*

Mountains and Music—Living Metaphors

Trained as a musician, I was immediately attracted to the
title of Mary Catherine Bateson's book *Composing a Life*. Although
I had never considered my life a work of art, I was intrigued by
the process of composing and creating a life. Creation and
creativity are linked as the way God acts in the world. The
creation as composition is the result of the creative acts of God
and the world.

I grew up in God's country, the mountains of Montana. God's
creation could be no better. I also spent formative years in musical
training. The living metaphors for my life were mountains and
sounds of music. From the intricate patterns on the veins of a
leaf to the sweeping sunsets, I've listened to the music of God's
spheres; I've heard the instruments of creation.

The years I spent studying music in high school and college
were the foundation of much of my life. I occasionally listened
to the improvisations of great jazz performers, but my favorite
musical compositions of my high school and college years were
the classics of Bach and Mozart. Whether I listened to or played
their compositions, the regular forms and conventional patterns
were comforting. Later, when I went to seminary, I decided to
study the flute again, this time just for the pleasure of it. My
teacher was the second chair flutist in the local orchestra. He
told me that being second chair gave him freedom to just play
the music, to enjoy the experience without the pressure of the
first chair. I thought he was a bit odd for not wanting to be first
chair, but now I salute his wisdom.

Studying the flute with him was not easy for me; it had
nothing to do with the difficulty of the music and everything to
do with the spirit of playing. I spent my time practicing mostly
Bach, Mozart, and a few French pieces. I remember one lesson
in particular. I could not, as usual, feel the style of the French
music. My teacher, after a frustrating moment, said, "You play

like a German: with precision, conciseness, and technical clarity."
I'm sure his comment was not meant to denigrate Germans, but
I could not play the style of the French music. He said, "Imagine
a summer picnic: gourmet food, good wine, relaxing by a scenic
river. Now, try the music again." The same fear that I'd had in
high school jazz band captured me. I was definitely more
comfortable with a Bach invention than with a French étude.
He had asked me to compose my life in new ways. I'm trying,
still. It's not easy.

I spent many summers hiking and backpacking in the
mountains of Montana and Colorado. Those summers that I led
backpacking trips as a guide, I always felt more comfortable
with my group of Minnesotans when we went on the established
trails up through the lake plateau country. I felt more secure as
we went up and down the switchbacks of paths that were well
traveled by others. But one week I decided to lead a group on
the other side of the river valley, a side that was less known and
less traveled. Some of the trails faded into the woods, and for
clues I had only the old blaze marks cut into the trees long ago.
Up above the timberline, near Coyote Basin, I could find only
the occasional piles of rocks, known as cairns. I felt less secure
and relied more on my group to watch, to look ahead, to be
aware. Sometimes we took wrong turns, ended up on tops of
cliffs, or backtracked. But I learned that summer to adapt to
new terrain, to adapt to and trust the group sense of where we
were. I learned to value the process of "getting there" as much
as the final destination itself. The mountains had taught me to
let go, to adapt, to improvise.

What I learned in the mountains of Montana has taken me
longer to apply to my personal and professional worlds. I want
to hold on to familiar and predictable paths through life. Mary
Catherine Bateson says that life itself is a work of art in process.
We find the "living metaphors with which we describe the world"
as we move through daily existence. My formative years were
shaped by those faint trails, by barely recognizable blaze marks,
by cairns standing in the distance, marking the way. I've come
to realize that the path is the point. Life, like hiking, is the activity
of adapting, of seeing new things, of trusting the familiar to
confront the new. The art of my life's composition has been

realized as the art of improvisation. This metaphor of "context, interaction, and response" is a difficult one to choose. It's much simpler to walk the familiar, well-traveled paths. But those paths never have led to the places that I long for, places that dreams are made of.

The creation of God, which I discovered in the mountains of Montana, has taught me that God's grace provides both the blaze marks and the fortitude to move ahead with others in concert. I have learned to connect with the group, look for the marks ahead, adapt when necessary, and welcome the new. I enjoy the trails when I let go into the timing of the wilderness. While the rocks of ages may not seem to move very far, they are part of a grander composition of freedom and novelty—of God's great improvisation on the notes of grace. God's grace is the unifying melody, which sometimes "provides background support" and sometimes "lets us fly free." Our vocation is to let go into God's grace, to adapt, to create, to improvise.

The improvisational nature of the Christian faith is masterfully captured in Patrick Henry's metaphor of the "ironic Christian."[2] To be an ironic Christian is to explore the "field marks of the grace of God." Henry doesn't produce a how-to-guide, but rather his insightful composition is one of showing the readers the experience of God's grace. The music is often disruptive, unexpected, surprising. Henry describes his project:

> This book is about the grace of God, but not about magic, and certainly not about something easy. It's about something simple, that God can be trusted but not taken for granted...The ironic Christian, who knows an "as if" world and the God who made it, certainly does not claim that all blasphemy is masked piety or that all Scripture must be taken with a grain of salt but does insist that very few answers are given in advance, and even those that are may not be easy to understand.[3]

God's grace is the music for the composition of the ironic Christian's life. The music does not always march ahead with predictable harmonies, forms, and rhythms. We feel the beat in places we least expect, interrupting the regular rhythms of our heart. We look for the field marks; we listen to the melodies. We listen to God's grace, trusting that God doesn't take us for granted.

After years of graduate work and teaching at a small liberal arts college, I realize that my desire to listen more to jazz and blues has its roots in my experience in the mountains of Montana. Although I still love the classics, I'm discovering a whole new kind of music that fits the feeling of being on the trail. It was in Montana that I learned to let go, to trust myself and the group, to look ahead and adapt. And now, in new and different ways, I'm learning the art of improvisation again, the art of "recombining partly familiar materials in new ways." Composing a life, as Bateson reminds me, is more like improvisation than following the predictable score.

Composition and Creativity

Creativity is the means by which God creates the world and the means by which we fulfill our destiny as the *imago dei,* the image of God. To be human is to create; it is our evolutionary calling. Works of art, poetry, and music convey the grandeur of our creative vocation. But we also are called to less spectacular endeavors—putting our daily lives together in new ways, transforming the old, challenging the status quo. In the mundane lurks infinite possibilities. I learned from a student of mine that instead of Descartes' famous dictum, "I think, therefore I am," we should identify ourselves by the phrase, "I create, therefore I am." We are by nature aesthetic. To compose is to create; to create is to live.

Creativity is the opening movement of our faith: "I believe in God, creator of heaven and earth." We commence our self-understanding before God (*coram deo*) within the wide arena of the cosmos. From images in scripture to the early church theologians' beliefs, tradition has developed the creativity of God's composition. We can find images of creation in Genesis 1–3, Psalm 8, John 1, Colossians 1, and many other places.[4] The doctrine of creation claims that the creation is good, that God is its source, and that all creatures depend on God for their existence. Why has Christian tradition neglected the composition of creation?

Too often Christian tradition has explained the themes of God's creation in static, ponderous categories: Not only did God create the world out of nothing; nothing new has happened since.

It is as if God's incarnation in creation and in the person of Jesus the Christ makes no new difference to us. We treat the contents of the faith like the stone tablets handed to Moses on Mount Sinai—as unbreakable rules set in concrete. "In the beginning..." becomes the warrant for justifying the status quo, for preserving the "way it's always been." Centuries can pass before the atrocities of one generation are changed by another. We no longer justify the slavery of people for our personal use, but in some traditions women are still not ordained because we have an investment in preserving tradition when change threatens the powers that rule. Simply preserving the past for its own sake can lead to domination. Tradition sanctions the unchanging, eternal truths that defend us from the ambiguity and flux of the world.

But we know that the world does not work that way. Sciences tell us that the world is changing rapidly, that we have developed from a complex, evolutionary history. Many of us will move several times to new locations, will hold different jobs, and will be in a variety of different relationships. Our personal experience tells us that our world demands new skills, new ways of thinking, though we doggedly try to live in the same old ways as if they were divinely ordered. Likewise, we need new rituals and stories to shape our self-understanding. The point of the doctrine of creation, however, is that God continually acts in and through us in new and amazing ways. God's relationship to the world is alive and changing. We are created in God's image, as co-improvisers of the creation.

Scripture and Christian tradition are rich with lively, interactive metaphors for God's relationship with the world. From the beginning of Genesis to the gospels and in Christian communities, beliefs about God's relationship with the world have been expressed in ways that made faith come alive. But we have turned models into idols, giving certain ones oppressive authority over others. Alfred North Whitehead, in his small treatise *Religion in the Making*, criticizes Christian tradition for its models of God as the divine "lord" and "master" that have been used by Christians for centuries to justify the enslavement of others. The institution is wed to the models of its theology. Feminist theologians join in this same criticism by linking the models of Father and King to the patriarchal structures that have sanctified the oppression and abuse of women. As Whitehead notes, "In Christian history, the charge of idolatry has been bandied to and fro among rival theologians. Probably, if taken in its widest sense, it rests with equal truth on all the main churches, Protestant and Catholic. Idolatry is the necessary product of static dogmas."[5] Our images calcify; the living God becomes the stone of our idolized words. We must find new ways to keep alive the message of God's grace by connecting it to the world in which we live. The challenge is to begin again— that is, to take those words from Genesis and translate them into living words that recreate the living relationship that God first established in the creation of the universe. We need new theological models that fit both the Word and our world. God's Word in creation and in Jesus the Christ is not a repository of static truths but an event that is ongoing between God and the world. The fit is between the Word, God's gracious, incarnate presence active in all of creation, and the world, a chaotic, shifting landscape of multiplicities. Creativity is God's gracious gift to us to shape and improvise on the creation in which we live. Faith is the art of practicing that gift, of fine-tuning the art of improvisation.

A model must be both productive and provocative. The model that I propose draws on the musical imagery of improvisation, particularly that found in jazz and blues. The creative art of improvisation provides an opportunity to re-vision the themes of God's grace in creation and redemption, the incarnation of Jesus Christ, and the way we live in this world. A common theme of this model is that the world in which we live requires that faith adapt and improvise on the music of creation. Before we continue to explore the model of improvisation, we must ground the composition of creation in the major key of God's grace. Like the twelve-bar harmonic structure of the blues, God's grace structures and shapes the music of faith.

The Music of Creation

Christians have interpreted and used the doctrine of creation in a variety of ways. In the early church, Irenaeus drew on the doctrine of creation to combat the gnostic heretics who claimed that the flesh was evil. Other theologians have viewed nature or creation as merely the stage on which the human drama of salvation takes place. How we perceive the composition of creation is essential to our understanding the purpose and meaning of human existence and God's relationship to the world.

The composition of God's creation is built on the theme of *God's grace*. From the grace inherent in nature to the inexplicable presence of God's grace in Jesus Christ, the *Christian faith claims that God's love is expressed in all of creation*. Paul, in his letter to the Romans, connects God's love to the suffering of the creation:

> I consider that the sufferings of this present time are not worth comparing with the glory about to be revealed to us. For the creation waits with eager longing for the revealing of the children of God; for the creation was subjected to futility, not of its own will but by the will of the one who subjected it, in hope that the creation itself will be set free from its bondage to decay and will obtain the freedom of the glory of the children of God. We know that the whole creation has been groaning in labor pains until now; and not only the creation, but we ourselves, who have the first fruits of the Spirit, groan inwardly while we wait for adoption, the redemption of our bodies. For in hope we were saved. Now hope that is seen is not hope. For who hopes for what is seen? But if we hope for what we do not see, we wait for it with patience. (Rom. 8:18–25)

God's grace working in creation is the theme around which all others revolve. From the creation's primordial beginnings to its ultimate endings, God shapes the movement, sustains its life, and gives it purpose and direction. Through the trinitarian movement of God's self, Christians have claimed that in Jesus the Christ all creation is created, held together, and reconciled (Col. 1:15–22). The composition begins ex nihilo and ends as new creation, alpha and omega. I will examine three theological voices that emphasize the primacy of God's grace in creation through Jesus Christ as the locus for human salvation: (1) the first article theology of Gustav Wingren, (2) Celtic theologies, and (3) feminist theologies.

Before listening to these three voices, however, we must note that Christian tradition has not always emphasized God's grace as the primary theme in the composition of creation. From the theology of Augustine to that of the Reformers, Christian theology in the West shaped the theme of God's grace primarily in anthropomorphic categories. The Barthian turn in theology in the twentieth century, with its radical call of God's grace to humankind in Jesus Christ, drove God's creation to the periphery. Karl Barth, sure that we do not obtain knowledge of God through nature, developed a radical polemic against natural theology. The primacy of revelation as a theological category in Barth leads to an epistemological priority of gospel over law. Neoorthodox theology became strongly christocentric, sometimes to the near exclusion of creation from the realm of God's grace. Similarly, modern existential theology from thinkers such as Rudolph Bultmann emphasizes radical individual human commitment to God, and nature is the "stage," so to speak, for human salvation and God's action in human lives. This is a radical departure from the "two source books," of Scripture and nature in the tradition of thinkers such as Aquinas and even Augustine. Yet there are voices whose primary movement is still creation.

Gustaf Wingren, a Swedish theologian opposed to the theology of Barth, is critical of the theological tradition that has neglected creation. For Wingren, creation is the Christian gospel's foundation, not an appendage. Why has the church neglected the doctrine of creation?

> Indeed, the doctrine of creation has not only been neglected; it has been the object of opposition since the 1920s, especially on the part of Karl Barth and his disciples. But the source of this negative attitude lies much farther back in time and is associated with the conditions under which Pietism and the revival movement arose in Europe. The roots of today's situation lie back in the 1600s, in the era of national churches and the absolutism of rulers.[6]

Wingren is particularly critical of his own Lutheran tradition, which sees a sharp antithesis between law and gospel, nature and grace. He notes that this had particular consequences when the pietists began to focus on Jesus alone. This emphasis has not changed much in many churches today. From the language of television evangelists to the popular piety in the pews, American individualism has cast God's grace in the shape of a "me and Jesus" theology.

As an antidote to this radical christocentrism, Wingren draws on the theology of Irenaeus as a voice in the early tradition who gives primacy to the doctrine of creation. "What is needed now is *a renaissance of Irenaeus.*"[7] With Irenaeus' help, we can refocus theology to emphasize that salvation is part of God's original plan. Irenaeus' theological battles were against the gnostics, who claimed that God could not have anything to do with the physical, material world. In contrast, Irenaeus reaffirms the goodness of creation and its fitness for God's incarnation. "Irenaeus begins with creation and then continues with the incarnation in the Son, in order that the whole may be seen as the restoration of creation (*recapitulatio*)."[8] Irenaeus draws together the three articles of the creed in one movement of God's grace. Like the movement in the sonata allegro form, the themes of creation are established in the exposition, convoluted in the development, and brought back again in the recapitulation. The music of creation shapes the movement of the gospel. The creed is shaped in the same way, refusing to separate creation from the gospel and from life in the Spirit.

Our current global crisis triggers Wingren's determination to reestablish creation as the foundation for the Christian faith. If social ethics are based on Jesus alone, our responsibility is only to serve the *human* neighbor. Wingren wants to expand this command to include all of creation. Love of neighbor encompasses the entire creation. "The western world as a whole gives the appearance of a single large super-class, ruthlessly using up the natural resources of the third world."[9] To reorient theology firmly in creation reorients the human task of responsibility in the proper sphere. We cannot act like the gnostics, who viewed creation as an unfit vehicle for God's redemption. Instead, we are called to cooperate with God in restoring and recreating nature. Wingren's theological voice challenges the radical christocentrism in theologies that limit God's grace to humans as if God could not save or be bothered with the rest of the creation.

The doctrine of creation establishes the elastic and expansive boundaries of God's grace. The message of salvation in Jesus Christ is centered in God's intentions for the created order. Philip Hefner measures the scope of God's grace:

> We are never "outside" God and the grace of God. God will use our lives, weak as they are, for the purposes of what really is. Christ's message is not that he came to pay our debt through his death, but rather that despite our sense of guilt and inadequacy, we have never been outside God's gracious ambience. The cross and death, far from paying some imagined debt, are instantiations of how life for us is to proceed, a project we are part of.[10]

A chorus of theologians—Philip Hefner, Elizabeth Johnson, Paul Sponheim, Joseph Sittler, Sallie McFague, and John Cobb—shift the tradition's center of focus to the deeper *cantus firmus* of God's grace in the whole of creation. Only then do the other themes blend with the harmony of God's intentions.

A second instance of these new and yet ancient voices is the resurgence of Celtic Christian hymns and spirituality. To be sure, a certain sentimentalization of Celtic Christian spirituality has grown parallel to its popularity. However, the early saints and monastic communities understood the limits with which nature bound their communities. Many early Celtic Christian writers identify nature as the creation of God and as a revelation and source of grace. They do not simply love nature for nature's sake, but always as a window to the Divine.

On a recent trip to England, my students and I spent a day tracing the sacred places of early Christianity. On a cold January morning we took a coach and drove out to Lindisfarne, known as Holy Island. Careful to watch for the time when the tide would return, we explored the edges of a barren and unforgiving landscape. Legends record the penitential experiences of Saint Cuthbert. He would stand in the turbulent, cold waters of the North Sea through the night and return to shore in the morning to be comforted and warmed by sea otters. The early island monastics, free of our twentieth-century prejudice about being separate from nature, did not romanticize the natural world. As Philip Sheldrake notes, "In contrast the Celts, whom we tend

to romanticize, simply *lived with* nature because they existed in
constant contact with it and could not afford to be disrespectful
to it."[11]

The famous hymn attributed to Saint Patrick lifts up the
themes of Celtic Christian theology:

> I bind unto myself today
> The virtues of the star-lit heaven,
> The glorious sun's life-giving ray,
> The whiteness of the moon at even,
> The flashing of the lightning free,
> The whirling wind's tempestuous shocks
> The stable earth, the deep salt sea
> Around the old eternal rocks.[12]

This hymn links the strength, power, and grace of God to the
strength, power, and grace of God's creation. The elements of
nature bear the presence of the Creator. Saint Patrick's hymn is
found in the baptism section of *The Lutheran Book of Worship*.
The trinitarian opening invokes the power of God in the life of
the believer, in the realm of the creation. The very water that is
sprinkled over the baby in baptism is the same water of the
"deep salt sea around the old eternal rocks."

Celtic spirituality, like many other creation-centered
spiritualities, could be one more way to sentimentalize our
relationship to creation. However, the popularity seems more
deeply rooted in a hunger among Christians to recover a theme
of God's composition that has been ignored. Philip Newell,
Warden of Spirituality and minister of the Church of Scotland,
writes about the characteristics of Celtic Christianity that have
sneaked through the dominant Augustinian tradition. Newell
claims that we need to listen carefully to the lost music of Celtic
Christianity so that we have a fuller composition of God's creation.
When we listen to only one voice, other subtle harmonies are
lost and the composition is impoverished. Newell follows the
voices of Celtic Christianity from the "heretical" voice of Pelagius
in the fifth century to the founder of the Iona Community, George
MacLeod, in the twentieth.

Newell contrasts the theologies of Augustine and Pelagius.
Those we have condemned as heretics may actually have much

to contribute to tradition's interpretation of God's grace in creation. Students of theology are usually taught that Pelagius discounted God's grace and claimed that we accomplish salvation by our own endeavors. This rash simplification is as misleading as thinking that Augustine considered the human being to be totally depraved. Newell reminds us that Pelagius' theology was considered dangerous because of its emphases on the fundamental goodness of creation, the original righteousness of humans (in contrast to an Augustinian notion of original sin), his concern for social justice, and his advocacy for the education and leadership of women in the church.

> There are two areas in which explicit criticism of Pelagius does begin to merge: his practice of teaching women to read Scripture and his conviction that in the newborn child the image of God is to be seen. These issues are clearly related, for the desire to educate women was rooted in Pelagius' conviction that God's image is to be found in every person, both male and female, and that the goodness of that image is nurtured and freed largely through the grace of wisdom.[13]

These themes draw on the Wisdom/Sophia tradition from the Hebrew Bible and from the gospel according to John. From the beginning, Sophia has empowered the creation and fed it through her goodness.

Roman Catholic feminist theologians sing the familiar, centuries-old refrain that all of creation is sacred and reveals the Divine. Elizabeth Johnson revitalizes Sophia (interchangeable with Wisdom), a feminine image of God, to express this conviction that all of life reveals the sacredness of God. Sophia, as the breath of God, creates and gives life to the world. "This creative function relates the Spirit to the cosmos as well as to the human world, to communities as well as to individuals, to new productions of the mind and spirit as well as to new biological life. All creatures receive existence as her gift, she who is named in the Nicene-Constantinopolitan creed giver of life, the vivifier."[14] Sophia is the divine creator of all life; the one who continually renews, replenishes, recreates the cosmos from beginning to end.

To correct the patriarchal deficiencies of classical theism, Johnson's development of God as *She Who Is* breathes life into the relationship between God and the world. Grounded in a strong trinitarianism, Johnson's development of Divine Sophia connects creation to the way that God is in God's self. Johnson explains: "Holy Wisdom does not exist in lifeless self-identity but corresponds to herself in a threefold repetition by virtue of which she can freely encompass the world. Unoriginate source, unknowable mother of all, she forever comes forth from hiddenness as her distinct self-expressing Word."[15] God's gracious way in the cosmos is God's gracious incarnation in humankind—liberating, renewing, recreating, moving, blowing.

Susan Ross develops similar themes in her work on a feminist Roman Catholic sacramental theology that begins with the sacramental principle that all of life is sacred and reveals God's presence. "According to the sacramental principle, human beings find God not by leaving or denying the world, but by becoming immersed more deeply in it."[16] She develops three implications of this sacramental principle: Creation is revelatory of God's presence; community is a fundamental category of relatedness; and the life of Jesus Christ is integral. However, Ross points out that sacramental life is inextricable from our finite life, which is by nature ambiguous. Thus, the sacraments as they point to God's presence are understood and interpreted as signs of God's presence in the culture and history of our ambiguous life. What follows in Ross's book is a critique of the patriarchal structure of Roman Catholic sacramental theology with a reconstruction of sacramental meaning in light of the experience and practice of women's lives.

Wingren's theology, the wisdom of Celtic spirituality, and feminist theologians remind those of us in the early twenty-first century that we may need to listen to new (and simultaneously ancient) music for the millennium. As we enter a new millennium, I cannot help but recognize both the power and the danger in the church's message of the gospel. If we remain entrenched in the same old themes of an individualized, personal relationship with God and ignore the rest of creation, we may find ourselves trapped in our own monochromatic melodies. We need new images, new voices, new music.

The voices that I'll be drawing on are those from the twentieth-century world of jazz and blues. The composition of creation is like the improvisation of a theme in jazz—resisting all efforts to be captured in one final form. The composition of creation, like the power of the blues, snares us into the music of the composer. Our hymns to the universe echo the words of Paul in Philippians: "So that at the name of Jesus every knee should bend, in heaven and on earth and under the earth, and every tongue should confess that Jesus Christ is Lord, to the glory of God the Father" (Phil. 2:10–11). In Christ, we hold to the promise that from the beginning to the end, all things are the composition of God.

Two Models: The Orchestration, the Improvisation

Christian theology articulates the doctrine of creation from many perspectives. Two fundamental ones are from the *archonic* and the *epigenetic* perspectives. Ted Peters, in *Cosmos as Creation,* explains these two views as metaphors in terms of which tradition has viewed nature and, consequently, God.[17] The *archonic* view proposes a "cosmic blueprint" or "score" in which all details are planned ahead of time. Everything in all its variation and novelty is planned from the beginning. This view corresponds to the "classical" model of music and to the relationship of the symphony orchestra and its maestro. The *epigenetic* view meshes more easily with an evolutionary worldview, in which change and movement to greater complexity characterize the natural world. As Irenaeus suggests, this view is also more faithful to scriptural accounts of God's ongoing action in the world. The model of jazz improvisation fits this view of God and the world and how we live in the world. Faith discerns the play between improvisation and the structure of the score. These two models need not be mutually exclusive, but tradition has often put them in opposition with each other.

The claims of faith must be intelligible and applicable to life in this world we call creation. Our vision of creation has to be in conversation with the context of what the sciences are telling us about our world. The rhythm of the natural world is the rhythm of God's creation. In particular, the image of creation and the ideas of complexity from science bring the theme of improvisation to life. Forming creative elements out of chaos and uncertainty is the very way improvisation works.

We are part of a cosmic composition in which all creatures in the natural world play their parts; the creation and redemption of humankind are the "refrain" within the larger composition of creation. What God is about in this world is accomplished through the natural world, through creation. Lutheran insistence that "the finite is capable of the infinite (*finitum capax infiniti*) is a statement both about the incarnation of God in Jesus the Christ and about God's incarnation in the created order.

The Orchestra

Classical music mirrors the theological world of classical theism. While this may be, of course, an oversimplification, the correspondence fits for many people's Christian piety, in which the God of classical theism still reigns supreme despite all the revolutions in academic theology. Viewed from this perspective, God resembles the conductor in tuxedo and tails who enters the symphony hall to direct the concert. Before the conductor ever arrives on stage, members of the symphony orchestra carefully tune their instruments, listening carefully for matching pitch and blend within their sections. Each instrumentalist carefully opens the music, mentally reviews the part, and awaits the grand entrance of the conductor. With a brisk walk and a gracious bow to the audience, the conductor picks up his baton, and the performance begins. Each individual note, phrase, and dynamic marking from cover to cover of the score is memorized. Music is created as each person plays his or her part, listening carefully to how it fits in with the other voices. At the end of the composition the conductor bows, the musicians rise, the audience applauds, and the newspaper critic heads out the door mentally fashioning a nasty review!

Anyone who has ever played in large classical music ensembles knows that the personality of the conductor shapes the music. The musician's role is to sublimate his or her own creativity and blend in with the ensemble. The success of the performance in large part depends on the cooperation of the musicians to fulfill each detail of the musical score. The music is laid out ahead of time, and the score is the blueprint. The conductor's job is to interpret the music and to direct the process. Little room is left for individual interpretation or spontaneity. Many classically trained musicians would say that there is much more to playing in a symphony than I have described, and I would agree. But the metaphor carries the idea many people have about how classical music performances take shape.

A story from my husband's high school band–directing experience illustrates this point. At a recent all-state band festival, the conductor had also composed a piece for the concert. Each rehearsal taxed the students' patience as he demanded that every detail of the piece be performed exactly as he had written it. This included the clarinet cadenza in the middle of the piece. Normally, a cadenza can be rather freely interpreted by the instrumentalist, which is exactly what the first clarinet player chose to do. However, the conductor stopped the entire band every time to inform her that she had misinterpreted one rhythm within the cadenza. Finally, after being yelled at continually, the clarinet player cooperated. The evening of the performance came, and the conductor began directing his own composition from the podium. Soon, however, my husband (seated in the audience) noticed that the conductor was trying to stop the band during the middle of the clarinet cadenza. The clarinet player, a young woman with a twinkle in her eye, proceeded to play the cadenza the way *she* had wanted to interpret it. And with a nod, after finishing the cadenza, she proceeded to lead the band into the next section of the piece. The conductor finally stopped waving his arms and succumbed to the student. In some traditions, this rebellion would be viewed as sin. However, that evening of the performance, she was a hero among the other students.

Some Christians, rooted firmly in the traditions of classical theism, describe the event of creation and God's role in a very similar way. "In the beginning…" is much like the opening notes of a symphony. God speaks, and the composition is created; each detail is planned ahead in all its infinite variety. Creation is a once-and-for-all act that occurred "back then," and we are now merely playing our parts that were planned ahead for us. Our role in this picture is to follow the score. God, the creator and source of all, is the one on whom the whole composition hinges. God is both the composer of the score and the conductor of the ensemble.

Ross plays out this image in her critique of the sacramental life. In examining the role of the presider during the eucharist, Ross notes that pre-Vatican II services did not emphasize the role of the presider but the function of the ritual. "The Mass was neither the possession of the clergy nor of the people: it was simply *there,* and everyone knew what was expected."[18] Vatican II reaffirmed the eucharistic celebration as *the* central focus of the liturgy, but though the Council insisted that the liturgy was the work of the people, the "official view of Roman Catholicism— without the priest, there is no real presence"— still dominates.[19] Consequently, the role of laity, particularly of women, continues to be subordinate to that of the priest. The eucharist, Ross says, developed into a "one-man show." Women are excluded not only from celebrating the sacrament but also from the language of the service itself. Many women have turned away from the official church to develop alternative worship practices. However, some have left the church altogether. They simply cannot go on "playing their parts" in the "one-man show."

Historically, the primary metaphor for the relationship between nature and God has been the image of the orchestra and conductor. With the advent of Einsteinian physics and evolutionary biology, the model of jazz and improvisation has come to seem more appropriate. Three models developed recently by thinkers in science and religion reflect the historical development of the understanding of the relationship between God and nature.

Three Theological Models

The use of these models illustrates the complex historical and cultural contexts in which the ideas of nature and God come into being.[20] "In each field new ideas were the product, not of isolated individuals, but of communities of inquiry within wider cultural contexts."[21] Both science and religion interdependently influenced each other's understanding of God, humanity, and nature. As Barbour explains, the social histories of science and religion help to situate our own contemporary understanding of nature, humanity, and God. He uses the language of competing paradigms (Thomas Kuhn) or research programs (Imre Lakatos) to explain our current worldview, in which no one paradigm has completely transformed our world.[22] Barbour explains that we live in a time of competing paradigms. In order to understand the new, we must explore the previous views. Our contrast and comparison of God's actions in the world of nature will help us connect it to musical analogies. Much like the role of God in the world, the role of conductor and the development of musical composition are paradigm dependent.

The Ancient Greek world draws on the thought of Aristotle and Plato to develop a model of nature as a "created hierarchy."[23] The center of this worldview was the earth, around which the other heavenly bodies—whose shape was "perfect and incorruptible"—revolved. This view became the foundation for the medieval view. Christianity dominated culture during the Middle Ages: It was the matrix for the development of the sciences, music, and the arts. The music of the time represented the science and theology of the age: fixity of the forms, the celestial spheres, a geocentric/anthropocentric worldview, and dualism. "In the twelfth and thirteenth centuries, *dualism* of thought and action eventually activated a powerful Gothic synthesis. This dualism, vividly predicting the future Renaissance, exhibited its polarity in many ways. In politics a struggle persisted between Church and state. In social life aristocrats and clergy faced a formidable adversary, the rising bourgeois."[24] Barbour notes that the analogy between nature and God was monarchical, like a kingdom. In contrast to the later deism of the Enlightenment, God's role was active and present, but all-determining.[25] The God of classical theism resembles this picture of God as the great composer/conductor. God's attributes are defined by absolutes: omniscience, omnipotence, omnibenevolence, everlastingness, creativity, immutability, and impassibility. Furthermore, the God of classical theism affects the world, but the world does not affect God. The relationship is one-directional. God's omnipotence means that God controls and rules the world in every way. God not only knows the future but has predetermined every event. To imply otherwise would be to say that God is not in control of the world. This model inspires a certain kind of worship, much like the orchestra's adoration of the charismatic conductor.

This model is complicated by the philosophical world that accompanies it. God's *eternity* was, of course, a biblical theme, and the human quest for the security of a permanence beyond change is a perennial one. But the exclusion of all temporality from God's nature seems to have been indebted mainly to Greek thought. Plato had pictured a realm of eternal forms and timeless truth, imperfectly reflected in the world; the perfect was the unchanging. Aristotle had spoken of God as the Unmoved Mover, the immutable Absolute.[26]

God's perfection was completely opposite of the world. What God is, the world is not. Whitehead explains by saying that God was the metaphysical exception to the world.

From the early Middle Ages to the mid-nineteenth century, one dominant model of how God created the world prevailed. Barbour examines the historical development of the relationship between God and nature through the rise of modern science.[27] Although modern science radically challenged the medieval view of God and nature, many presuppositions of this world-view dominated the Christian doctrine of creation even into the twentieth century. Saint Thomas Aquinas' marriage of Aristotelian philosophy and biblical theology combined ideas into a tight, coherent system with persuasive power that lasted well beyond what we call the Middle Ages. Rooted in his view of the natural world is a corresponding view of God rooted in classical theism. And Aquinas' classical theism is resonant with the music of his time.

The most important music of the day was sacred, especially in the service of the mass. The forms of music, like the places of the celestial spheres, were fixed for eternity by God's hand. The quality of perfection, whether applied to God's power and existence or to the places of the planets in the universe, was marked by a contrast between what God was (perfect) and what the creation was not. Even the compositions of the time, particularly sacred music, utilized the perfect intervals of the overtone series (fourths, fifths, octaves). Dissonance was carefully "controlled and disciplined," using the second, sixth, and seventh intervals.[28] Music, theology, and science were in an intimate relationship. Barbour notes that the medieval worldview "was not greatly altered by the Reformation in the sixteenth century but…was to be drastically transformed by the impact of modern science."[29] However, changes that began in the Reformation and Renaissance would have a lasting impact. Again theology, science, and music were intimate partners, reflecting cultural shifts. Although liturgical music was still dominant, composers during the Renaissance turned to secular compositions and created new forms to reflect the individualism of the period. Science was also reflected in the musical composition:

> Scientific inquiry led to curiosity and investigation, both encouraged in the humanistic Renaissance. This scientific spirit also affected music. The art of counterpoint—writing polyphonic music—became so highly developed and refined during the sixteenth century that the rules then established for writing this music are studied by twentieth-century composers.[30]

With the upheaval of the Reformation, "all the western world seemed to be agitating—politically, religiously, economically, scientifically, philosophically, socially—propelled by an urgency that left in its wake tension, paradox, intensity, and a restlessness that often pushed men to extreme limits."[31] The Baroque era was the source for Bach. The developments that began in the theology of Luther and the science of Galileo were ushering in a new age. These years were the beginning of the era known as the Enlightenment. Gillespie notes that Baroque music reflected the drama and urgency of the time period. Baroque music became known for its exciting rhythms, sense of drama and flamboyance, increased use of dissonance, and a cultivation of new forms. What was the role of the conductor and composer?

The second model begins in the Renaissance/Scientific Revolution, coming to fruition with the Enlightenment. This view of nature, associated supremely with the brilliant synthesis of Newton, understands the world to be deterministic, explainable by mechanical causes. Change occurs in nature but is still viewed as rearrangement of forms already established. There is no real novelty. This reductionist, dualistic worldview sees nature as a machine and God as the creator of the machine. It is known as the argument from design, and William Paley draws an analogy between the universe as a watch and God as the watchmaker. A verse from a poem by Robert Burns summarizes the mood of the Enlightenment, the Age of Reason:

When Nature her great masterpiece design'd,
And fram'd her last, best work, the human mind.
Her eye intent on all the mazy plan,
She form'd of various parts the various Man.[32]

Gillespie notes that music lags behind the other arts in the eighteenth century, and so the golden age of Classicism in the arts does not occur until later in the century. Classical music reflects the philosophy of the Enlightenment, the Age of Reason: pure taste proportion, restraint and constraint, skepticism of religious authority, deism, and a universal trust in the human spirit and human reason. Gillespie quotes Mozart: "Passions, whether violent or not, must never be expressed in such a way as to excite disgust, and as music, even in the most terrible situations, must never offend the ear, but please the hearer."[33]

The Romantics disliked the mechanical model. Essentially German in origin, the Romantic movement was a reaction against the ideology of the Enlightenment. Nature was appreciated for its own sake, not for its machinelike regularity. Gillespie explains:

> While the Romantics were acutely aware of the mystery in the universe, they could not agree with the Deists that such a universe was a machine and that every natural phenomenon could be rationally explained. Preferring to meditate on the mystery of creation, and rejecting harsh reality for the gentle world of fantasy, emotion, and religious sentiment, the Romantics felt a spiritual tie with medieval legends and culture, Gothic architecture, and the mysterious Orient. Exoticism was an inevitable by-product of this turning away from reality.[34]

Nature's beauties were expressed in the music, poetry, and art of the Romantic period. One can read the poetry of Wordsworth or listen to Berlioz to understand this contrast to the Classical period. Freedom of expression was valued above the restraint and regularity of classical compositional techniques. Yet Gillespie notes that these composers still "intended that their inspiration should be governed by universal rules of form and structure."[35]

The third modern model is developed in science from Darwin to the New Physics. Music, philosophy, and the other arts reflected the revolution that was happening in science. With Darwin's theory of natural selection, the worldviews of both the Middle Ages and the Enlightenment were threatened. In Darwin's theory, nature is viewed in an evolutionary perspective: Order is emergent; law and chance shape the structure; life is relational, ecological, formed by systems and wholes, multi-leveled, and communal in relationship.[36] The relationship between subject and object changes drastically from the Enlightenment. What were assumed to be separate are now viewed as intimately related. One's perspective shapes the nature of reality. Anton Webern, a twentieth-century composer, writes, "Anyone who assumes that there's an essential difference between consonance and dissonance is wrong because the entire realm of possible sounds is contained within the notes that nature provides—and that's how things have happened. But the way one looks at it is most important."[37] From chromaticism to twelve-tone music to aleatory music, the repudiation of traditional concepts occurs in almost every form of music. With the birth of the new science comes the birth of multiple forms of music and multiple theological forms. The very way music is composed and performed is challenged.

From our brief discussion of these models of God and nature, we can see that our self-understanding is not simply pre-determined in the past by some divine fiat. We are developing through time in relationship to the history of where we have been and the future of what is yet to be. Hefner is critical of the notion that our human identity was predetermined and that we just fulfill what is given to us:

> Human nature was not defined and fixed at some point of origin in the past. Whatever we were in the primordial past, we are not that now. Nor will we be the same in the future. Our essence is yet to be determined. Our nature is dynamic. And the dynamism comes from the eschatological future…in shaping the passage forward toward God's own *telos* or purpose which will appear in its fullness at the consummation, at the final perfection of the whole cosmic history of the creation.[38]

We understand ourselves not only from our past but also from our future. Our future is drawing us into who we will be. Our past does not determine the present or the future. What was begun in creation moves somewhere, goes places, does things. We know who we are by how we become. But many of us were taught to see our endings like our beginnings, as primeval places of perfection. Eden foreshadows Eternity. We want to return to the mythical garden where life was once perfect. But this is where our interpretation of our myth of origin fails. We have never been in that past perfect place. Yet the Christian would surely claim that there is a falling. For our entire history points not to what "should be" but what "should not be."[39] Where we started and where we are going are not the same destiny. As Douglas John Hall explains, our falling is precisely our failure to trust to accept the movement of God's grace. "The temptation of Adam and Eve and of the Christ, the temptation of Everyman and Everywoman is to *have* their being rather than having to *receive* it."[40] Instead, we are called forward to find our home in a future of God's that was established first in the opening notes of creation and brought to fulfillment in the life of Jesus Christ. God's creative work is also God's redemptive work as we are brought into the future of a new creation.

The Improvisation

Jazz has been the showcase for modern forms of improvisation. However, improvisation was not born in the twentieth century; it developed in many ways and in many different contexts. Jazz is one expression of improvisation. Gillespie comments on the origins and development of improvisation:

> As we know, improvisation is not new. Two thousand years ago, improvising on established melodies was a common practice among the Greeks. During the Middle Ages, singers improvised countermelodies against a given melody. Renaissance musicians accepted improvisation as a natural part of performance, and by the Baroque era it had become a fundamental part of performance. Thus improvisation has had a long and steady history.[41]

Jazz differs in some ways from other compositional arts. Jazz players are composers, in a sense, as they create the music within the ensemble. The composition is not handed to the ensemble merely to be repeated in performance. The performance becomes the composition in process. "Simultaneous improvisation can be an exciting experience for musicians and listeners: the various players in the ensemble listen to each other and converse in musical dialogue, all the while preserving harmonic unity."[42] The composition of improvisation is a musical dialogue. "Jazz is not jazz until some transformation or improvisation takes place."[43] The composition takes place within the ensemble—co-created by the performers.

Jazz emphasizes the relationship between the individual and the group. In contrast to classical Western European musical ensembles, jazz showcases each individual's unique talents while the ensemble as a whole offers support. This contrast is characterized in a quote from Max Roach:

> When a piece is performed, everybody in the group has the opportunity to speak on it, to comment on it through their performance. It's a democratic process, as opposed to most European classical music in which the two most important people are the composer and the conductor. They are like the king and the queen. In a sense, the conductor is also the military official who's there to see that the wishes of the masters—the composers—are adhered to, and as a musician your job may depend on how you conform to the conductor's interpretation of the composer's wishes. However, in a jazz performance, everyone has an opportunity to create a thing of beauty collectively, based on their own musical approaches.[44]

The power relationships are changed and even inverted in a jazz ensemble.

The metaphor of improvisation is helpful for addressing the reality in which we live and for moving us beyond the limits of the traditional doctrine of creation. Stephen Richter compares the aesthetic worldview of Euro-American classical music and the essence of jazz and blues, particularly in the works of Thelonius Monk. He claims that Western music views composition as a closed process, a work that is created by someone with a master plan, with a "creator's blueprint."[45] His view is quite similar to that of Ted Peters, who calls creation *archonic*, the cosmic blueprint model.[46] Our role in this model is to live out the intentions and plans of the creator. The beauty and essence of the composition remain essentially unchanged.

The aesthetic model of jazz and blues, in contrast, creates the piece from the players. Richter speaks of dialogue, of a developing conversation. Compositions are not spoken into existence with a single word, but are created through dialogue. "It is not the monologue of one composer or conductor using his musicians to realize his vision of the master plan. Also, it's a dialogue not only of the four players, but also of their particular histories and traditions."[47] The aesthetics change, and the goal of the composition changes. Jazz and blues offer an alternative way of playing the music, of creating the composition. The composition is woven from the structures of the piece and from the interaction of the players. The leader does not dominate the group, insisting it be played his or her way. The composition is built along the way; it becomes a project that is creative, cooperative. In a world where there isn't one universal voice, or one song, the image of blues and jazz offers an alternative way of creating and playing the compositions of God. Our role is that of the created co-creator.[48]

Creating compositions in jazz and blues has an element of chance or risk that occurs among the players. Because the musicians don't simply play the same notes all the time, the composition continues in new and different forms. This element of the composition conforms to the qualities of the evolutionary world in which we live. We know that the world is not made by simple fiat, that the species are not fixed, and that change is part of the way nature works. One could argue that chance is not part of the cosmic blueprint; chance threatens the omnipotence of God. On the other hand, one could show that "evolutionary science deepens not only our understanding of the cosmos but also of God…When we think about God in the post-Darwinian period we cannot have exactly the same thoughts that Augustine, Aquinas, or for that matter our grandparents and parents had. Today we need to recast all of theology in evolutionary terms."[49]

Some theologians immediately rule out any notion of chance operating in the cosmic order because it would violate the attributes of classical theism. However, other contemporary theologians do not immediately rule out chance as though it were necessarily a contradiction to who God is and the way God composes the world. Feminist theologians and scholars involved in religion and science are recasting the doctrine of God in such a way as to incorporate and even enhance Christian belief in the bargain. If God's power is domineering, like that of a monarch or lord, God would be expected to control the whole show. On the contrary, if divine omnipotence is recast as persuasive love, God's power is more mutual, allowing for the creation's own composition. John Haught explains the connection:

> A God of love influences the world in a persuasive rather than coercive way, and that is why chance and evolution occur...If God were a magician or a dictator, then we might expect the universe to be finished all at once and remain eternally unchanged...God is not a magician but a creator. And this God is much more interested in promoting freedom and adventure than in preserving the status quo. Since divine creative love has the character of letting things be, we should not be too surprised at evolution's strange and erratic pathways. The long struggle of the universe to arrive at life, consciousness, and culture is consonant with faith's conviction that love never forces but always allows for the play of freedom, risk and adventure.[50]

God's loving freedom creates the composition of creation with its creatures.

Elizabeth Johnson offers this metaphor of improvisation that combines scientific understandings of chance and law:

> God is like a master theatrical improvisor in live performance, amplifying and embroidering each theme as it presents itself; like a choreographer composing steps in tandem with the creative insights of the whole dance troupe; like a composer of a fugue, starting with a simple line of melody and weaving a complex structure of endlessly folding it back upon itself; like a jazz player, inspired by the spirit of the audience and the night to improvise riffs upon a basic melody; like a designer who sets the rules of a game that includes wild cards and then lets it play.[51]

This model connects to her notion of God as Creator Spirit. Likewise, the spirit of creation embodies the attributes of God. In this picture, God is the supreme exemplification of the creative act. God works with the world to develop the composition. Improvisation is creation through God's creative and redemptive action in the world. Creation is an ongoing process enacted in the relationship of God and the world. The composition of creation is God's creative improvisation on a world created in freedom through love.

HOW WE perceive the composition of creation is essential to our understanding God's relationship to the world and the meaning and purpose of human existence. In a world where there isn't one universal voice, or one song, the image of improvisation in jazz and the blues offers an alternative way of creating and playing with the composition of God's creation.

2

CREATIVITY AS CREATURELY VOCATION

Instead of worshiping ancestors or deities conceived as parents, we must celebrate the mysterious sacredness of that which is still to be born.

MARY CATHERINE BATESON[1]

WHEN FACED with the chaotic and turbulent in our world, how do we respond? We must find ways to uncork the creative potential of humankind as transformative agency for the betterment of all creation. Creativity is God's gracious gift to humankind for shaping and improvising with the creation for the purpose of living a fuller life. Creativity is our creaturely calling.

Who We Are and Where We Are Going

As we enter into a new millennium, we ask, Who are we as humans? Anxiety and the technological complexities of Y2K brought out the best and worst in the way many of us prepared for the new epoch. Our own technological wonders that save and preserve lives daily were also threatening to bring about disaster by the means of terrorists or through the meltdown of computers at the fateful hour of midnight on December 31, 1999. Media hyped people to anticipate the worst and spend thousands of dollars on generators, freeze-dried foods, and gallons of water. Some bought guns to protect their goods from possible intruders. Cult leaders proclaimed the end of the world. Preachers warned of the impending wrath of God. I must admit to having a couple of extra gallons of water in the house. However, most of my own fears were wrapped around the way we had anticipated the worst and prepared for it—by caring only about our individual survival. What does this say about the way we face our future? What kinds of strategies do we rely on when disaster looms, when fear threatens our well-being?

A strange thing happened during the transition between December 31, 1999 and January 1, 2000. The computers kept working; no terrorists blew up anything; and the world watched another day come and go. Our worst fears expired; life continued as usual. For many in the world, the millennium was an invention of Western culture and Christian theology. Time passes differently for others. And yet the Western world, with its technological power and its religious traditions, however attenuated it has become, has snared others into its worldwide web.

Yet I found myself doing the one thing I had not anticipated doing. For almost twenty-four hours, I sat spellbound in front of my television set, as ABC broadcast each New Year celebration from around the world. Fireworks exploded, and people opened champagne. Partway into the millennium celebrations Peter Jennings switched the broadcast to a small camp of Somali refugees in an African village of tents. No fireworks, no champagne, just the quiet stillness of people awaiting another day just like the one before had been. I thought of my own comfortable home, where I sat watching the drama of the world around me unfold, and I felt a sickness in my stomach as I thought about how many people panicked about Y2K disasters, oblivious to this small refugee village in Africa. Life without material pleasures, which is an abstract fear for many in the United States, is a daily reality for millions of people in the world. I wonder what this new millennium will bring for those people. Will the rest of the world, including me, realize that the power of this network drama of the New Year was not in the champagne or fireworks, but in the connections made between the parts of the world whose lives are filled with suffering and desperation? This drama of the New Year connected my part of the world with theirs, if only for one brief moment of time.

We can respond to the unknown, to the future, to the unexpected with fear, or we can learn to adapt in innovative, creative, life-giving ways. Some people responded to the new millennium with a sort of desperation that tried to make some coherent sense out of rapidly changing events. Others awaited God's wrathful destruction of the world, knowing that they would be spared and taken away to heaven. It is clear to me that we have both the gift and the responsibility to handle the future that God has given us. When faced with unexpected, unfamiliar, even fearful situations, many of us respond with what has always worked, with what is familiar. But it seems that the world is changing more rapidly then we are ready for.

The power of this millennium media event was evident in the sigh of relief that passed through an entire world, relief that we had survived, that life was going on into a new future. This sigh of relief is a kind of grace note that gives us a moment to reflect on who we are and where we are going. We have choices: We can continue with the fireworks and champagne; we can hunker down into our bunkers of fear; or we can cross into the worlds of those whose lives are not our own and face the future together. I keep thinking that if humankind has the intelligence to remedy computer systems around the world, we must have the gift to adapt our skills to problems that threaten the well-being of the world. What would happen if we put the same energy we put into Y2K into feeding the hungry, clothing the poor, visiting those in prison? We need a new understanding of who we are and what our purpose in life is.

Some visions of the human that are being preached from pulpits reinforce the understanding that humans are here on earth only to depart for their true mission in life in heaven. Dorothee Soelle comments:

> Many Protestant denominations deny human beings the power
> to imitate God in doing justice. Instead of celebrating our
> participation in creation, Protestantism emphasizes the
> unchangeability of the world and human sinfulness. Many
> Protestant theologies have concluded that we cannot change
> because we are so evil and because we have no power. This
> deprecatory talk cuts us down and severs us from faith and
> participation in God's good creation.[2]

In this frame of mind, we cannot move beyond simply "playing
our part," and when the music changes, we don't know how to
adapt. As in the image of the "Maestro" and symphony developed
in the first chapter, we have been trained to simply follow the
Master, unaware of our own gifts and abilities. This image no
longer works. We must find ways to uncork the creative potential
of humankind as a transformative agency for the betterment of
all creation. What would happen if we listened to the grace
notes of God, which lead us to the music of creative vision, of
finding new ways, of adapting the old to the new? We might
understand ourselves differently, tell a different story.

The stories we tell about ourselves reveal our self-
understanding. What is our identity and calling in life? How do
we understand the notion that we are created in the image of
God (*imago dei*)? Creativity is the God-given vocation of all
creation, especially humankind. Creativity is God's gracious gift
to humankind for shaping and improvising on the creation for
the purpose of living a fuller life. The first story that gives shape
to creation is from Genesis, in which God's creative act gives
shape, pattern, and meaning to the flux of chaos. Christians have
explained their destiny within that story. And now, Philip Hefner,
says, "Planet earth has reached the point where the success of
human beings in actualizing who we are—*self-aware creators of
culture*—is critical for the entire planetary ecosystem, including
the planet's nonhuman inhabitants."[3] Our beginnings connect
us to our future.

Improvisation as creativity is characteristic of the way both
humans and nonhumans work. Creativity is the matrix from
which the play of creation continues. Like improvisation in jazz,
creativity is the process by which the new is created from the

patterns of that which is given. To examine the nature of creativity, I will use the works of four scholars: Alfred North Whitehead, a process philosopher; Mihaly Csikszentmihalyi, a psychologist at the University of Chicago who has devoted his career to studying creativity from an evolutionary framework; Mary Catherine Bateson, an anthropologist and author; and Philip Hefner, a Lutheran theologian. Although each thinker has different emphases, they are similar in their explanation of creativity as a complex process that involves the interplay of novelty and order, ensemble and individuality, stability and flux.

In chapter 1, I suggested that the model of jazz provides a helpful metaphor for explaining God's creation of the world. In the creation of the world, God endows the creatures with God's image—to create. Creativity is our natural vocation—living out God's will in freedom for continuing the work of God in creation. As we noted before, God does not simply create the world with one divine fiat, but is continually creating and making all things new. Therefore, to understand our creaturely vocation of creativity is to understand God's purpose for us in the world. By exploring these four individuals' descriptions of creativity, we can relate our creative acts to the creative actions of God. Six ideas emerge from the four thinkers: (1) Creativity is an aesthetic process to create and perceive the beauty in God's creation. (2) God as Creator creates what is natural in us, our own idiomatic parts. (3) God works *in* creation and is not some additional force outside the world. (4) God creates *with* creation. Creativity is a relational, systematic activity, not just an individual phenomenon. (5) God's gift of creativity carries an inherent risk. (6) Creation is about hope for the future. The creation is free to use, or not use, creativity for the betterment of others.

Mary Catherine Bateson—Learning Along the Way

Mary Catherine Bateson has been my guide on an absorbing journey, offering rich metaphors for navigating my way through a crazy, topsy-turvy, spinning world. In a world marked by rapid change, diverse cultures, and expanding technologies, Bateson's work provides strategies for negotiating this postmodern landscape. She claims that *how* we learn relates to *what* we learn. Instead of simply clinging to one tried-and-true way of being in the world, Bateson teaches her reader how to learn in new ways, how to see things in new ways. She leads her reader through stories in a myriad of places that link multiple perspectives. The reader learns to look for new patterns in the familiar, old patterns in the unfamiliar. Bateson offers learning strategies for making one's way through the kaleidoscope of an interdependent, multidimensional world:

> Ambiguity is the warp of life, not something to be eliminated. Learning to savor the vertigo of doing without answers or making shift and making do with fragmentary ones opens up the pleasures of recognizing and playing with pattern, finding coherence within complexity, sharing within multiplicity.[4]

Underneath her writing is a profound optimism that life is a place where we are always learning. She uses many different metaphors to explain this lifelong educational process. We learn through the metaphors and stories we construct to make sense of our world. When we retell each other's stories, we make connections between the familiar and unfamiliar.

Bateson explores the metaphor of improvisation in *Composing a Life*. "Life is an improvisatory art, about the ways we combine familiar and unfamiliar components in response to new situations, following an underlying grammar and an evolving aesthetic."[5] She examines the lives of five women who creatively worked through the possibilities and difficulties their lives presented. This study of improvisation is a study of creativity. Each woman discovers the patterns along the way instead of conforming to a predetermined essence. In a stable, homogeneous society, where everything fits neatly together, the typical artist creates something in a traditional, formed style. Bateson, however, is addressing a different world, one where "the materials and skills from which a life is composed are no longer clear."[6] Bateson uses an analogy from music, particularly that of jazz musicians. Jazz exemplifies a kind of creativity that holds together the individual and community, freedom and constraint, structure and chance. Improvisation helps us deal with the ambiguities life presents because it helps us confront the unfamiliar with the familiar, the chaotic with order.

In her book *Peripheral Visions*, Bateson reaches deeper into this model of improvisation and connects it to the theme of vision. How we look at the world will shape how we cope with the world. If we look at the world through a single-vision lens, we miss those things in our peripheral vision. We are blinded to the diversity, multiplicities, and ambiguity within our range of sight. Bateson develops this metaphor extensively in a chapter called "Improvisation in a Persian Garden." She explains how single models, that is, a sort of "visionary reductionism," don't fit the complexity of life's landscape. "Openness to peripheral vision depends on rejecting such reductionism and rejecting with it the belief that questions of meaning have unitary answers."[7] In our rapidly changing world, we can no longer see through just one lens, especially if we think that it is the only one through which everyone should look. Instead, we must learn to see multi-dimensionally, to live with competing visions, to explore new ideas. We live this way in concert with others.

Learning is the art of improvisation. Learning and improvisation share the same qualities for those who are open to the world around them:

> Improvisation and new learning are not private processes; they are shared with others at every age. The multiple layers of attention involved cannot safely be brushed aside or subordinated to the completion of tasks. We are called to join in a dance whose steps must be learned along the way, so it is important to attend and respond. Even in uncertainty, we are responsible for our steps.[8]

We are held responsible as lifelong learners in a constant process of creative discovery. We are responsible for how we learn what we learn and what we do with what we know. Knowing and doing, epistemology and ethics, are connected.

Bateson's own background brought her to many cultures and different peoples. Her family, both when she was a child and later, after she married, lived all over the world. The temptation would be to think that her multicultured, well-traveled worldviews are a matter of privilege. To some degree this is true. Yet whether we live in rural South Dakota or London,

England, we all face how we deal with the differences in our complex world. We are no longer exempt from the possibilities and problems that diversity brings. Many think there are only two options: We can deal with diversity by running from it, shoring up the defensive walls and hunkering down, or we can assume that truth is determined merely by one's personal taste, and relativism rules in its anarchic way. Those are our fears, yet we all live with commitments. How can we live in a committed manner and yet be open to the voices of those who are different from us? Is there a third option? Answering this question is part of Bateson's task. Improvisation is a creative solution to this dilemma. What we learn to do is to maximize diversity instead of minimizing it. Thinking we are all alike is a kind of homogeneous imperialism. As we live and work together, we realize that differences do matter. But they can matter for the good. The improvisational model moves us away from warlike metaphors that pit one against the other, an "us-them" attitude. "It is curious that the sins of disobedience against God have been emphasized so much more than the sins of hatred between brothers."[9] Bateson's genius is her emphasis on creativity. To learn is to create in partnership and through difference.

In a similar manner, Alfonso Montuori, an educator and musician, develops the theme of improvisation as a metaphor for the learning community. He is critical of the way academic communities stifle creativity and set up barriers to genuine collegial dialogue. The academic world has often modeled itself as a battleground where scholars compete to outdo one another's theories. Competition instead of collaboration is the means by which learning takes place. This battleground means that we are afraid to sound ignorant, afraid to show that our models might not be the final truth:

> In public, in journals, conferences, and presentations, we generally present our models, theories, and methods but do not account for the complexities, ambiguities, and uncertainties which preceded them. In public, we show what we know, and what we do not know becomes minimized, obscured, defended, feared, a source of embarrassment: We are afraid we may have missed something, that we will be caught with our pants

down, unable to answer the pointed question, locate the vital
reference.[10]

Many of us have made presentations at conferences where the
whole agenda was to try to shoot holes in the presenter's paper.
Academics are trained to shoot down their competitors, not to
collaborate. Once we find teaching positions, we attend
conferences and write grants about collaborative learning.
However, our entire academic process has worked against the
kind of creativity that leads to fertile collaboration with other
colleagues. The lone scholar myth still pervades most graduate
schools.

Montuori challenges this model of learning and offers an
alternative metaphor. His own background in music leads him
to the theme of improvisation. He finds rich resources in the
works of African American theorists, who have been critical of
European music. Jazz provides an alternative way to think about
creativity in contrast to the tight, precise, and controlled music
of many Euro-American composers and musicians. Jazz focuses
on a community of conversation, in which the give-and-take
creates ongoing fresh statements. "In jazz, spontaneity,
improvisation, ambiguity, uncertainty, and even mistakes—
particularly mistakes—are used as avenues for new explorations
and also as a testament to the improviser's ability to think on
his/her feet."[11]

Montuori applies the musical model to the academic
community. For knowledge to be creative, one must be willing
to take risks in a trusting community. The old "battleground"
model wages war and reinforces distrust among colleagues. The
jazz model encourages trust, community, and an enthusiasm for
the process of creating music together. Montuori notes that he is
not calling for abandoning high standards for intellectual rigor,
but is calling for a different way of going about it. "Creative,
collaborative inquiry is in some sense the delightful shadow side
of the instrumental, technological, self-contained knowing."[12]
Learning in this kind of system will feel risky; we will "expose"
our weakness at first until we learn to trust those around us. But
when we do, the spirit of collaboration will allow for a new kind
of work, a different kind of creative spirit. Montuori and Bateson

both encourage work that is not only creative but also and necessarily transformative. Creative work leads to the transformation of knowledge and the learning process.

Flow: Mihaly Csikszentmihalyi

Mihaly Csikszentmihalyi, a professor of psychology and education at the University of Chicago, has spent his life studying the process of happiness and creativity. His studies define his conception of "flow": that experience of losing oneself to a creative process.[13] Flow is not an elitist concept reserved for the brilliant artist. Like the music of jazz, flow is the music from beginning to end, the reason one plays. Csikszentmihalyi's methods lead him to research in many cultures, in many different kinds of social and vocational settings. The emphasis of flow is on the process, not just on the end result, the product. He explains that many psychologists have studied the aberrant personalities, the psychotic, the despondent. But how are we to learn about that which gives life, that which perpetuates the good, if we only study its opposite? His research goal to study creativity is to study that which creates happiness, that which produces life and well-being.

To define creativity, Csikszentmihalyi doesn't ask what creativity is, but instead explores *where* creativity happens. He dispels the myth of creativity as the process of a lone, crazy, individual spirit. Creativity is a social phenomenon occurring within systems. He notes, "Creativity does not happen inside people's heads, but in the interaction between a person's thoughts and a sociocultural context. It is a systemic rather than an individual phenomenon."[14] Creativity is a social process that requires a social context. Likewise in jazz, creativity is a way of life, a preoccupation of the artists. Paul Berliner explains: "When performers speak of jazz as a way of life, they refer to the performer's constant preoccupation with musical ideas and notions of creativity…they refer to Barry Harris's students continually reviewing music history while riding on the subway…they refer to Lee Konitz whistling new melodies to the beat of his footsteps as he walks his dog in the evening."[15] Creativity occurs within the natural rhythms and happenings of everyday life.

Three major components are required for creativity: the domain, the field, and the individual.[16] The domain "consists of a set of symbolic rules and procedures."[17] Domains can be separate fields of knowledge, such as religion, math, legal systems, or physics. Each system has its own rules and symbols. Domains belong to the realm of cultural evolution. The field is necessary to determine whether or not the novelty produced will become part of the dominant culture. Csikszentmihalyi notes that a culture can only absorb so much new information, and, consequently, cultures are conservative by nature to assure their own survival. Thus, competition exists between memes (discrete units of cultural information).[18] A field is a way of passing judgment that determines whether or not the creative innovation will survive. He defines a field's makeup as a group of "experts in a given domain whose job involves passing judgment on performance in that domain. Members of the field choose from among the novelties those that deserve to be included in the canon."[19] Fields can use narrow or broad filters and encourage novelty when they are culturally appropriated. Finally, one must consider the contributions of the individual person. Yet, even in this discussion, creativity is still seen as a property of the overall system. The person making the creative contribution must internalize the domain within which he or she works, understand the criteria of judgment, and relate the work to the larger culture. The systems model of creativity has important implications: "The level of creativity in a given place at a given time does not depend only on the amount of individual creativity. It depends just as much on how well suited the respective domains and fields are to the recognition and diffusion of novel ideas."[20]

Csikszentmihalyi's description of the creative person is developed from many interviews and has much in common with the jazz musician, whom Red Rodney describes: "You keep playing, keep studying, keep listening, keep learning, and you keep developing. Jazz is not a nine to one [a.m.] job, once or twice a week. It's a way of life."[21] The creative process, as Rodney sets it out, resonates with what Bateson and Montuori said. "Creative individuals are remarkable for their ability to adapt to almost any situation and to make do with whatever is at hand to reach their goals. If nothing else, this distinguishes them from the rest of us."[22] The creative personality is *not* the lone, crazy individual working in splendid isolation. From many interviews of scientists, artists, and writers, we come to know the creative person as one who has access to the domain, to the field, and is open to the twists and turns of experience. The creative person is finally a complex person, one who exhibits the contradictory extremes in life and brings them together in fruitful possibilities. Csikszentmihalyi lists ten sets of opposites that embody the creative personality.[23] For example, creative individuals have a great deal of energy, and yet they also know when to take time to be alone and rest. Developing the creativity within oneself depends on practicing the art of careful attention to the environment. Creative acts do not come de novo, but often as the result of hard work, attention to detail, timing, and some element of luck.

Csikszentmihalyi's description of the creative person is much like Whitehead's notion of creativity, in which the many become one and are increased by one. Creativity is the creation of that which is new. Csikszentmihalyi notes,

> Creativity involves the production of novelty. The process of discovery involved in creating something new appears to be one of the most enjoyable activities any human can be involved in.[24]

In earlier works, Csikszentmihalyi described this experience as *flow.*[25] Whitehead is famous for his methodological airplane ride in which he explains the creative action as a combination of particularity and generalization. The play of free imagination is grounded in the details of observation. Whitehead explains that "the true method of discovery is like the flight of an aeroplane. It starts from the ground of particular observation; it makes a flight in the thin air of imaginative generalization; and it again lands for renewed observation rendered acute by rational interpretation."[26] The imagination brings the familiar into new territory. We see the familiar in new ways. Creativity is an evolutionary process in which the past unfolds into the possibilities of the future through the reality of the present.

Csikszentmihalyi explains that creativity used to be the domain of the gods. Humans were weaklings subject to the whims and tantrums of the deities. But somewhere along the way the scenes changed, and the humans became the creators, the gods. Creativity is our evolutionary calling. "It is not surprising that as we ride the crest of evolution we have taken over the title of creator."[27] Whether our destiny will be our fall is yet to be seen. But we bear an ultimate responsibility for how we use this gift. "It's a random coupling of behavior type with a feeling, which over time achieved a greater survival or reproductive advantage. And now we are in a sense 'designed' to want to be in flow."[28] We are designed to be creative; we feel good when we discover something new. Novelty is necessary for the future of who we are as a species on this planet.

Csikszentmihalyi claims that we construct our future through the creative process of flow. Our future is emergent, not predetermined in the past. We discover who we are along the way. "Individual enjoyment seems an evolutionary potential in humans, responsible in large part for technical and social advances, in future-oriented goals. It's intrinsic interest that keeps people going."[29]

Process as Creativity: Whitehead and Cobb

Bateson and Csikszentmihalyi confirm the notion that creativity is the means by which each of us lives out our evolutionary calling in life. Both authors agree that to understand the process of creativity is to understand how we develop worthwhile strategies for living in the world. Creativity is a social process in which novelty arises from that which is given. With some traditional theological perspectives, we have feared that by attributing creative power to humans, we diminish the creative power of God. However, my theological claim is that creativity is not solely the work of God. The rest of creation shares in the ongoing creative act. Process theology, along with other contemporary voices, such as feminist theology, challenges this notion that God's creation is a divine fiat that happened only once, only "in the beginning." In a way similar to process theology, Dorothee Soelle claims:

> We are mistaken if we assume that the life of the creator diminishes as "the created" live more fully. The power of life

is not a flat sum that must be divided, unequally, between the creator and the created, although the mainstream theology often conveys this strange impression. On the contrary, the more a person develops her creativity, delves into the project of liberation, and transcends her own limitations, the more God is God. God does not cling to creational power, making it his possession, but shares it knowing that good power is shared power.[30]

Whitehead, whose work is foundational for process theology, emphasizes creativity as the means by which God and the world are related to each other. Whitehead's vision of the relationship between God and the world is similar to the vision of the jazz ensemble, in which power is mutually shared, creativity is intrinsically related to freedom, and the creative process is as important as the final product.[31] Creativity in Whitehead's system, like a performance in jazz, resists being held captive in a final form. God is continually creating life anew.

A brief explanation about Whitehead's life helps to explain the origins of his philosophical works. His life and work reflect the goal he envisioned for all of life: to live and to live well. In 1890, Whitehead's marriage changed his outlook on life. He remarked about his wife, "Her vivid life has taught me that beauty, moral and aesthetic, is the aim of existence; and that kindness and love, and artistic satisfaction are among its modes of attainment."[32] This love of the aesthetic informed his primal vision of God and the world. For Whitehead, Christianity was not assent to correct doctrine, but a way of life that evoked meaning and concern. Whitehead feared that Western theology had so aligned God's power with brute force that the persuasive power of beauty and grace had been eclipsed. For Whitehead, beauty is the creative expression of God's imaginative power to transform death into life, old into new. God does not fight force with force; "he does not create the world, he saves it: or, more accurately, he is the poet of the world, with tender patience leading it by his vision of truth, beauty, and goodness."[33] Although some have criticized this vision of God as sentimental, Whitehead's correction of divine power as coercive fiat deserves attention again in a world marked by ugliness and manipulative, coercive power.

Of the three traditional metaphysical values— goodness, truth, and beauty—Whitehead chooses beauty as the ultimate value for life. This choice of beauty, as Whitehead notes, "somewhat shifts the ordinary philosophical emphasis upon the past. It directs attention to the period of great art and literature, as best expressing the essential values of life."[34] Creativity is that universal that applies to all of life. To create is to love beauty. Beauty lures us into the goodness and value of the creation. Dorothee Soelle calls Christians to participate in this aesthetic education:

> To love creation means to perceive its beauty in the most unexpected places. An aesthetic education that deepens our perception is not a luxury for the elite but a cultural necessity for everyone. To believe in creation is to perceive and to engage in the aesthetic model of perception...We become better lovers of the earth when we tell the earth how beautiful it is.[35]

When we see the creation as beautiful, we look at it in new ways, with new possibilities. To engage in that which is beautiful is to become part of the imagination of God. To create is to be in partnership with God to create that which is new. Jazz musicians sense this creative partnership when they enter into something that is "the big picture." The music carries them into another world, where "they feel a deep sense of reverence for 'all living things.' In spiritual communion, they merge together in the shrine of a universal life force—timeless, peaceful, yet energizing and euphoric."[36]

This principle of creativity and beauty is used in the contemporary theological writings of John B. Cobb, Jr. Cobb uses the philosophy of Whitehead to develop his theological understanding of the relationship between God and the world. Cobb's work is particularly helpful because he explains creativity within an aesthetic framework as the means by which God acts in the world. Cobb's book *Christ in a Pluralistic Age* connects the metaphysical principle of creativity to his vision of Christ as creative transformation. Using the work of Andre Malraux, Cobb traces the visual representations of Christ throughout the history of art. "Here there is a striking movement from radical transcendence through incarnation to crucifixion and assimilation through suffering humanity."[37] This tour through the history of Western art demonstrates the inextricable relationship of the present meaning of Christ to the interpretative history. Cobb demonstrates that the Christian may discern Christ as creative transformation in the changing styles and forms comprising the forms of Western art. Like the author of Colossians, Cobb identifies Christ as the one in whom all things cohere, the one in whom "all things were created." Christ himself is the process of creative transformation and cannot be identified with one absolute image. Creative transformation is the living image of Christ's presence in the world.

Cobb's christology, in a way similar to Bateson's, addresses the postmodern concerns of relativism, pluralism, and secularism. The language of christology must include not only "theological" vocabulary but also the terms of the world in which it lives. Cobb's theological language makes contact with both God and the world because christology is the focal point around which the meaning of God and the world ultimately matter. A postmodern christology can have nothing to do with a doctrine that imperialistically ignores the world in which it was formed. God's grace is at work in all the world and not apart from the world.

Cobb's christology addresses a world that converses in multiple conversations rather than in homogeneous monologues. Cobb's efforts in interreligious dialogue support his christological formulations. The best way to approach interreligious dialogue is through a christological formulation that not only acknowledges multiple conversations but also affirms transformation of those involved through the conversations. Like Bateson, Cobb opposes those who reduce Christianity to a single essence, to a single narrative. Many centers of meaning exist in the world. Cobb comments in *Christ in a Pluralistic Age* that "Christ, as the image of creative transformation, can provide a unity within which the many centers of meaning and existence can be appreciated and encouraged and through which openness to other great ways of mankind can lead to a deepening of Christian existence."[38] Christ, as the principle of creative transformation, excludes dogmatic finality and yet does not give in to a relativism lacking content or norms. Christ is the center around which other centers find a new and deeper meaning. In the language of jazz, unity is found amidst the diversity of styles. "Similarly, as music systems around the world provide jazz performances with additional sources of inspiration, improvisers may have the sense of participating in a global discourse among music thinkers, negotiating musical ideas that transcend cultural and historical boundaries."[39] Creative moments in jazz, according to Berliner, inspire a humility that "envelops the artists in the grip of such awe-inspiring aspects of creativity" that the musicians renew "their sensitivity to life's spiritual qualities and great mysteries."[40]

However, Cobb fears that many people in our world are facing a great spiritual and moral crisis; they are apathetic to the environmental, economic, political, and cultural forces that threaten to destroy the planet. Cobb describes this world as one that is constantly on the brink of facing its own self-destruction. How do we begin to address this crisis? In his essay "Christ Beyond Creative Transformation," Cobb notes that theological thinking can begin from several starting points. One could begin with the historical Jesus, with the preaching of the early church, with christological debates of the early centuries, the doctrine of God, or recent christologies. However, all these ignore the urgent context of the world, which the word must address. Cobb begins with salvation as the starting point for christology because the problems raised in the postmodern world are so urgent.[41] The word must be able not only to address the world in speech and deed but also to transform the world. The most comprehensive and responsible place to begin is with the nature of salvation for the entire creation. The questions of salvation are too pressing to ignore. Note Cobb's emphasis:

> We should not use the symbol *Christ* for anything less than the power that works savingly in this comprehensive way. *Christ* must be the life that struggles against the death-dealing powers that threaten us and the way that leads through the chaos of personal and global life to a just, participatory, and sustainable society in which personal wholeness is possible.[42]

The symbol of *Christ* is a "living" symbol.[43] We crucify this living symbol when we limit it to common or proper nouns that reduce its soteriological function beyond the redemption of the entire world. As Gregory of Nazianzus, the Cappadocian, said, "What is not assumed, cannot be healed."

Christ is that symbol that works in a comprehensive way against all "death-dealing" powers; Christ brings life and hope for all creation. In an unpublished paper entitled "Postmodern Christianity in Quest of Eco-Justice," Cobb explains that the worth of all creation is the joy God experiences. He obscures the distinction between humans and other creatures to explain the benefits of salvation: "But God and the created order in their intimate connection constitute the context of all our thought and life."[44] Salvation is a participatory process including God and the world in which all work together for well-being, vitality, and enjoyment. Cobb's understanding of salvation results from his choice of beauty as the ultimate principle in life, for all of creation has intrinsic value. Creation has benefit and value not only as it relates to others but also in its relations to itself and before God. The intrinsic value of each created entity is "enjoyed" by God.

The purpose of Jesus as the Christ is not only to reveal how God works in the world but also to be the one through whom the new force of creativity works in all the world. Jesus Christ becomes the principle of creative transformation, the one through whom all things are made whole and well. Jesus Christ is God incarnate in the world, whether the world consciously recognizes it or not. In an article titled "The Presence of the Past and the Eucharist,"[45] Cobb shows how Jesus is specifically present in the eucharist and also present in all creation. He shows how the past is efficacious in the present. The sacramental presence of Christ affirms that God's transformative and gracious power is effective in all creation, in the finite stuff of the world. The sacraments are particular expressions of God's universal love and presence. The principle of creative transformation is at work in the world regardless of its being realized. This can be illustrated in Janna Tull Steed's comment about the music of Duke Ellington, whose music has been labeled "sacramental."

> Duke Ellington has been blithely called a cultural icon. The word "icon," in its original sense, refers to a prayerfully created and dedicated work of art, a picture or an image through

which the divine nature or word can be mediated to the viewer. As such, the image is no longer a lifeless object, but one animated by a living spirit. In this sense, Ellington is an icon. And his music is sacramental, too; because it is also a mediator of life-giving spirit. His art unveils the glory of what is luminously holy, but hidden, in the material world and in human flesh.[46]

God's grace is manifest in all of creation. This theme of God's grace is improvised on as creatures develop the theme through their own freedom. Like the music of Ellington, the life of Jesus unveils the glory and grace of God. Christ is the sacramental presence that names that which is salvific to the community of believers. The purpose of Christ for the world is more than revelatory, that is, to show the world what God is accomplishing. In other words, Christ does more than demonstrate or illustrate to the world what it already knows about God. Christ transforms the world.

These christological images of hope and salvation, whether transcendent or immanent, move the world through ambiguity and death to meaning and life. For the vision of the kingdom brings present injustices to light and "supports the claims of the weak and the powerless."[47] The way that Christ works in the world is through the valley of the shadow of death, through those historical structures riddled with ambiguity. God in Christ accompanies the world through the valley of the shadow of death. However, Christ is more than just a friend on the way. Christ is the one through whom transformation and new life occur. But this transformation always occurs through the ambiguity, not by avoiding it. This is the risk of the creative advance in which God and the world participate. Thus, Christ is not only creative transformation but also the suffering one through whom all cohere and have their end. Christ offers the world hope.

Cobb equates faith in Christ with hope in the future. The past, present, and future are not separable from one another. Their relationship constitutes Cobb's understanding of the role of the future and hope. "Jesus opens us to the present working of the Logos by assuring us of our future."[48] Christ is not to be identified idolatrously with particular results or accomplishments of the past. Christ corrects this distorted view of the past in order to "remove the obstacles to faith as openness to creative transformation."[49]

The structures of hope are none other than the structures of creative transformation. Whitehead's theme of adventure is evident when Cobb explains that the problem of our contemporary culture is not that we "believe too much but that we do not believe enough."[50] The structures of hope are formed when eschatological images "break courageously into transcendence."[51] These structures of hope are not merely wishful thinking but are grounded in the possibilities of the present world. The ordering of the possibilities comes from the transcendent Logos. Thus, the structure of hope is "the incarnation of this Logos whereby it is the effective structuring of actual experience. Hence, the structure of hope is Christ."[52] Creative transformation is the reason for hope, because it is at work everywhere in the world, confronting the negative with possibility. It is that "whose nature it is to bring into being just that which cannot be predicted until it occurs."[53]

Christ is the central image of hope, incarnate in the world. Images of hope that guide humanity into the future must not only have the possibilities presented through creative transformation as the Logos, but they must be grounded in the actual existence of the present moment. These images are at once transcendent and immanent. They are incarnate; they work from the present into the future. The task of Christians is to conceptualize images that do not return idolatrously to past images or look hopefully to some supernatural forms that are not grounded in reality. The task of finding images of hope is a large one for the Christian community, and Cobb gives criteria for naming these images of hope. These are the four criteria for calling an image one of Christian hope: (1) The image must be a recent product of creative transformation, not simply a resuscitation of old images; (2) the image must be reformable through a continuing process of creative transformation; (3) the image must be open to the process of creative transformation in the present; and (4) the image must have arisen through encounter with Jesus' words or as a result of immersion in his field of force.[54]

However, no new orders of liberation or images of hope ensure a utopian future. At the very heart of reality is "always the dream of youth and the harvest of tragedy."[55] The creative advance brings "decay, transition, loss, and displacement."[56] Tragedy is marked by what has been along with what was not and what could be. Ambiguity is inherent in the structures of reality. At the heart of nature is ambiguity. Hope lies in peace, in Christ as the truth, in the one in whom all things come together. Christ, as truth, is the imagination of God that inspires within us the hope that something lies beyond the bondage of our own vision. And yet hope is only possible as it is incarnate in the lives of individuals. Incarnate hope lives in the world, in the present moments of daily life. Hope lives from this world into the next world, where it receives its ultimate fulfillment. Thus, in Christ as the way, the truth, and the life, God is both the lure of possibility and order and the one in whom all comes to fulfillment.

Hope in God through Christ inspires the world as music inspires the performer. Jazz artists develop the growth of their creative potential over an entire lifetime. From this life of creativity comes a moral obligation to share their talent with others. The survival of music is grounded in the present spirit of the players. In a commitment to share with others, jazz musicians offer a vision of hope for the musical world:

> They hope to make their mark on a world plagued by social conflict and preoccupied with materialistic values. Improvisers view performance as a positive force that can redress this imbalance, if only in a small way, by replenishing the earth's soundscape with music possessed of beauty and vitality, integrity and soul to remind listeners of these finer universal expressions of human aspiration.[57]

To improvise on Whitehead's language: "God is the improviser of the world, with tender patience, composing it with her vision of truth, beauty, and goodness." Our role is to be part of God's imaginative soundscape of beautiful music.

Created Co-creator: Philip Hefner

Theologically, we take account of the two-natured human animal who is both conditioned and free by asserting, first of all, that *the human being is created by God to be a co-creator in the creation that God has brought into being and for which God has purposes.*[58]

Philip Hefner develops an understanding of creativity that is rooted in the Christian doctrine of creation viewed from an evolutionary perspective. Hefner, setting forth his agenda in *The Human Factor,* tries to make sense of the contents of the Christian faith in light of contemporary sciences. The central questions for Hefner are, Who are human beings and what are their purposes? To answer these questions he draws on theologians like Irenaeus, John Hick, Ralph Burhoe, and Joseph Sittler. Using Imre Lakatos' philosophy of science, Hefner constructs a project that works around a core hypothesis with auxiliary hypotheses. His main task is to present theological proposals for discussion. "What is essential is that the proposal appear to be interesting and fruitful for exploration—fruitful above all."[59] Hefner's method is one of the great strengths of his theological proposal. The strengths of his theology are in the fruits that it produces. Hefner's theology is not confined within the walls of ecclesiastical domains but encompasses human identity situated within the vast cosmos of God's creation. Hefner takes the world seriously as the place for theological reflection.

The core of his proposal, the theory of the created co-creator, becomes grist for the theological mill. We are created by God as creatures and simultaneously endowed with the responsibility and gift of freedom to co-create the world with God. The primary shape of Hefner's proposal provides information for humans to work with as they struggle in life-and-death situations on this planet. Hefner provides a narrative of self-understanding from the Christian perspective that will help humans to live "wholesome" lives and be responsible for the creation around them. Hefner's non-dualistic framework joins what much of the Enlightenment has put asunder: nature from culture, humans from technology, religion from science. He says, "my view holds that both humans and technology are parts of nature."[60]

We understand who we are in relationship to the cosmos in which we live. Creation is both creation out of nothing (*creatio ex nihilo*) and continuing creation (*creatio continua*). Nature is the birthplace of human understanding. In a rather interesting reversal of metaphors, Hefner describes our "place" in the following way:

> Our lives are not so much a traveling through nature's space and time, as if we were making progress on a journey or conquering obstacles in our way towards a destination that is important to us, as they are stations on a journey whose traveler is something that transcends us, and for whom still more stations lie beyond us. We are not so much moving through and over nature, as we are natural creatures who represent a discrete station on nature's way. We are not sovereign over nature, but rather an occasion with nature's sovereignty.[61]

Our journey is not from this place to another, as if the goal of faith were to leave where we were created. Our calling in life is to be located in this place God put us, in the garden. To find our niche in nature is to find our theological placement and self-understanding. We find ourselves already in relationship with the natural matrix that gave us birth. Nature is the place where we discover the sacred.

We are created co-creators rooted in our evolutionary history. "We are, first of all, thoroughly natural creatures. We have emerged from the natural evolutionary processes."[62] Hefner draws on a biocultural model that emphasizes our two-natured character as human beings. We are developed from our inherited genetic data. Also creatures of culture, we construct frameworks of meaning in order to understand who we are and to assess the world around us.[63] The evolutionary process is the means by which God created us as free creatures. We are dependent on God and the evolutionary past from which we came. Thus, we are "created." Yet we are not destined to be determined by our genes, and we are free creators with God. Freedom is both the condition of our existence and the means by which nature is "stretching itself" toward that which is new.

Christ is the one who embodies true humanity. Hefner, along with other theologians, shifts the primary focus of redemption to creation. In other words, the doctrine of redemption only makes sense if it is viewed in the large focus of the doctrine of creation. Nature and grace are not separate but are resolved in the understanding of the purpose of God in Jesus Christ for the benefit of all creation. In Christ, we know who we are and who God is for us. Hefner believes that we have the possibility to develop a new phase of evolution. In Christ, we find out what it is and who it is that God intends for us to be. "Jesus Christ becomes the central event for understanding what it means for humans to be God's proposal for the future of the evolutionary process."[64] In sacramental language, Hefner claims that it is precisely nature that is a fit vehicle (*finitum capax infiniti*) for God's grace. This is preeminently understood in the incarnation of God in Jesus the Christ.

If we understand that nature is the vehicle fit for God's grace, we must have a corresponding theological interpretation of humanity's relationship to nature, particularly in a scientific and technological age. As noted before, many theologies and Enlightenment philosophies bifurcated nature from technology and humanity from nature. Hefner's proposal offers a more helpful way of interpreting how humans are situated in the natural world. He develops a theology of *techno-nature* that corresponds to his anthropological notion of the created co-creator. Humans are placed firmly within the evolutionary process, and, consequently, technology is viewed as "natural." However, this is not to assume that Hefner is uncritical of humans' use of technology. On the contrary, he urges critical responsibility in our use of and discernment about technology. Concerns of social justice, war, and destruction are the ethical frameworks for comprehending this connection between techno-nature and the created co-creator. "Technology must be interpreted; it is a behavior to be guided; and it must interface in a wholesome or well-synchronized manner with the full range of earth's physico-biogenetic information systems."[65] Like the other voices analyzed in this chapter, Hefner links our ability to survive in the future with our ability to further our creative endeavors in ways that are wholesome and life-giving for the planet.

We are drawn into the future of what we will be. God is not finished with the world yet. We participate in constructing a world that is more wholesome for the entire cosmos. "The essential *humanum* that is emerging is being continually called by its destiny, and our ability to participate as an ordained co-creator is the result of the creative thrust of God."[66] We are not yet who we will be. God is drawing all the creation into a new destiny. What this means for Hefner is that God's creative work is also God's redemptive work. Our work as co-creators is part of God's redemption and re-creation of all of life. Our vocation is linked to the future of all creation. Our identity was shaped by the evolutionary history of billions of years, and our destiny is tied to that very same process through which God works. God's future is our future; we are not on the journey, but God's journey is moving through us.

Where Do We Go from Here? God and the World

We can summarize what we have learned about creativity from the authors we have studied. Like the musicians in a jazz ensemble, God works *in* creation and is not some additional force outside the world. Images we have inherited from classical theism or from movies where the "force" is operative "outside" the world are corrected by these authors who affirm that God works creatively within the world. Elizabeth Johnson, feminist theologian, puts it this way: "Nor does the Spirit's dynamic power arrive as an intervention from 'outside,' but is immanent in the world that is becoming."[67] God is not some additional force we add to the world; neither does God merely "intervene" from time to time as if looking down from above and occasionally deciding to enter worldly affairs. This deistic language of God's intervention, however, is part of many Christians' vocabulary. Deism seems to imply that God is only occasionally at work in the world, and only in those prime times when God finds it convenient. But the Christian doctrine of creation contradicts this notion by claiming that God is always at work in the world. This accent of *creatio continua* provides a counterbalance to the notion of *creatio ex nihilo*. New things continue to happen, improvising on the familiar to create the novel.

Johnson derives three insights from attributing creativity to God the Spirit. First, the Creator Spirit is immanent in the historical world. God and the world mutually dwell in and with each other. Second, God's creative action is also the re-creating and redeeming action of God. Creation gets a fresh start. On a daily basis we are called to die and rise within the baptismal waters of the cleansing created order. Third, the changing nature of our world implies that the Spirit does move within the world, making all things new.[68] Within a trinitarian framework, Christians know that God is immanently at work in the world. In a distinct move away from the classical theistic notion of God separate from the world, panentheism (God-in-the-world) identifies God at work in the entire cosmos.

Does God's creative work really make all things new? This eschatological promise holds possibilities for us in the present. The future of God also tells us about our past; where we are moving to shapes where we have been. Hefner uses the example of the train moving through the stations. We are not on the train; we are one of the stations through which God's creative action is moving. Johnson supports Hefner's image:

> The long and unfinished development known as evolution testifies to just how much novelty, just how much surprise, the universe is capable of spawning out of the pre-given order or chaos. In every instance the living Spirit empowers, lures, prods, dances on ahead.[69]

Even those Christian theologians who criticize process theologians for their metaphysical embrace of the creative advance must acknowledge the biblical evidence that points to a Creator God who is continually at work in the world.

God as creator creates what is natural in us, our own idiomatic parts. Bateson and Csikszentmihalyi emphasize creativity as a life learning process that is unique but also responsible to and within the community. God's view of the world is particular to each individual event and person. What God creates in us is unique to us. We become who we are through the relationships we have, from the background around us, and from the vision God inspires in us. What we do with our individual gifts carries an ethical responsibility. Creative expression is not confined to the paints of the artist or to the steps of the dancer. Each of us has been called by God to live creatively and responsibly in our world. Theologically, this creative expression is our calling, our vocation. We create where we are in daily living. Cobb defines this notion of call as an expression of God's grace working within the individual. How we take that call of God into our own life frees us to be in community with others.

God creates *with* creation to bring about that which is new. Creativity is a partnership of sorts. Hefner's notion of the "created co-creator" has inspired some to claim that this is theological egotism. To somehow claim that we are in partnership with God is to deny our status in life. However, Hefner's intention is to claim the opposite. The accent of being called into a partnership with God is to emphasize the enormous responsibility that our creativity entails. We are first and foremost ones who are created. We are thoroughly dependent on God for our existence, for our very life. But in turn, God has given us the gift and task of using our freedom to create the culture in which we live.

God's gift of creativity carries inherent risk. Hefner reminds us that the way the world has been created raises both theological and humane questions:

> To empirical observation, the processes of natural selection seem to be without overall purpose or meaningfulness and they appear to be replete with what humans consider to be evil, pain, injustice, and disregard for persons. Theological tradition places such issues under the rubric of theodicy, which refers to efforts to resolve the problem of how evil and suffering are to be related conceptually with the belief in a good and powerful God. For the theologian, nowhere do the problems of theodicy bear down with greater weight and urgency than in the consideration of the processes of natural selection.[70]

Hefner clarifies, however, that most philosophers and theologians have ignored the relevance of this issue to the standard question of theodicy. Some theologians will promise eternal bliss in payment for the pain suffered in this life. Humans will find their reward apart from the rest of creation. Again, such inattentiveness to the evolutionary processes seems to be rooted, in part, in a narrow focus on God's redeeming grace to the human world. If, however, as we have suggested, we begin with the doctrine of creation, we must claim that God's business of saving and recreating reaches to the entire universe.

Hefner develops the work of John Hick (based on Irenaeus) to find a means by which to deal with natural selection and the evolutionary process. Hick develops the language of freedom within the divine/creature relationship as the framework for interpreting evil. This freedom is inherent in all of creation. Unlike the process framework, God is not limited by the world or by the metaphysical principles, but is self-limited (*kenosis*). God's volitional self-limitation allows "breathing room" for all creatures. The world becomes new through its enactment of self-determining freedom and God-given space to grow. Freedom is inherent in the universe and is essential to the creative process.

From process theologians to Hefner to Csikszentmihalyi, all agree that the evolutionary process requires freedom. "Furthermore, we recognize in this interpretation that freedom did not emerge abruptly with the human species, but that its necessary and enabling conditions are deeply rooted in all of physical and biological reality, as the theories of quantum physics and chaos, for example, demonstrate."[71] This freedom is constrained by the limits of the past, by the environmental conditions in which it thrives, and by the abilities and choices of the creature. Creativity shapes the world's processes as it grows, changes, and matures. However, things can go wrong. With the risk of freedom comes the ambiguity of its use. How we live with this ambiguity is related to how we trust God's will for the world. The world provides much evidence to the contrary of a divine beneficence. God's creation looks at risk. Surely, we cannot discount or trivialize all the death that has already occurred in the past. We cannot simply write it off as mere chance if we assume the direction, will, and love of a Creator. What can we say? The creatures are free to use creativity or not for the betterment of others. Creativity gives life.

Creativity is ultimately about hope. I can think of no works of humankind other than the great creative achievements that give me hope about the world and God's intentions for it. Creativity is a reminder that the process is bigger than we are. Creativity is a communal process involving self and other, God and the world. Bateson's profound optimism gives us hope that, even amidst profound loss and despair, the human spirit can learn and change its circumstances:

> If it is true that the unit of survival is the organism plus its
> environment, a sensitivity to the environment is the highest of
> survival skills and not a dangerous distraction. We must live
> in a wider space and a longer stretch of time. In thinking

about survival, we must think of sustaining life across generations rather than accepting the short-term purposes of politicians and accountants.[72]

To survive is not enough, however. God calls us to flourish in this world that was given to us. To flourish is to create together. We can be hopeful because we are aware of our responsibility for the long haul. God's creative work in the world will not end with this generation. From millions of years to greater epochs to come, God's will is for all creation. Our hope is God's hope. The future is God's creative action for us and for the universe. Our note of grace from God is that we are freed for our neighbor to do more than simply "play the part." We are freed to improvise new music, to dance new steps, to create new stories about who we are and where we are going.

CREATIVITY is God's gracious gift to humankind for shaping and improvising with the creation for the purpose of living a fuller life. Creativity is our creaturely calling.

3

PERFECTING THE ART OF "HANGING OUT"

A jazz band is an expression of servant leadership. The leader of a jazz band has the beautiful opportunity to draw out the best of the other musicians...But the effect of the performance depends on so many things—the environment, the volunteers playing in the band, the need for everybody to perform as individuals and as a group, the absolute dependence of the leader on the members of the band, the need of the leader for the followers to play well. What a summary of an organization!

MAX DE PREE[1]

WE ARE a people struggling to find community amidst the diversity in our world and the complexities of our scientific and technological advancements. How can we not only survive but live well in this world? We can practice the art of "hanging out." We become who we are through the relationships we develop over time.

We Are Who We Are with Others

When I was in high school, the cool kids (at least in my life) hung out in the band room. Band produced its own kind of culture, where students gathered together during their free periods to practice, to visit with the band director. Some of my best learning occurred in these casual, informal opportunities, when the time for playing music was less structured and I could take greater risks. Even the band director seemed to relax. Mr. Wickham seemed more friendly and more open, even taking out his clarinet and playing along with us. Now in my professional years of teaching religion in college, I realize the value of those times when we perfected the art of "hanging out." Many of my best friends were musicians, and I still keep in touch with some of them. This musical culture of hanging out helped to nurture creativity in many of us who otherwise might have been intimidated in the larger, formal settings of concert band or orchestra. Similar learning happened for friends of mine in theater, athletics, and speech.

When my mother and some of her friends reached retirement age, they decided that they would perfect the art of hanging out. Friendships deepened over long lunches at local restaurants, during aerobics at the fitness center, and over discussions of favorite books at their church quilting sessions. Like the musicians in the high school band room scene, these women learned from each other through casual, informal, interactive times when mutual ideas were shared. Many of my teaching colleagues could learn from these senior women. We have lost the art of hanging out, of taking time to just be and learn with each other. My life seems to run to the contrary, where time for just relaxing and letting down is at a premium, and I use my "breaks" to collapse after a busy semester.

This last year many of my friends and I struggled with professional issues of staying where we are or moving on to new opportunities. After applying for and being offered interviews for several jobs, I decided that my interest in moving had less to do with dissatisfaction with my job and more to do with something deeply spiritual that I could not articulate. I took the time to think about my motives for moving and why I might want to stay put. I talked to colleagues, gathering their opinions to help with my own decision. The decisions were never clear. I couldn't figure out what I wanted. Then one day after a colleague from out west came to spend time with me, I realized that her comments began to shape my decision. She commented on how lucky I was to have such wonderful, rich friendships. These friends, I realized, knew how to hang out. While all of them are involved in important professional settings, they all value time for conversation, for relaxing, for hanging out. I knew that some of my deepest insights about my theology and teaching had been nurtured in our casual conversations over lattes at the local bookstore. This community of friends was becoming more important than my need to move on professionally. I know now that to be creative, I need the rich, fertile ground of friends and colleagues who provide the safety of a community in which I am loved and nurtured. I've chosen to stay, for the time being.

Our times are complicated and chaotic. We struggle with ways of being together as citizens of a pluralistic, multifarious, and busy world. Many families can't find time to eat dinner together; students are so busy working they don't have time to learn. We measure our success by the hours we clock. We work harder and faster so that we can take what few hours are left in the day to relax. However, we defeat our own goals. Usually, we are too tired to relax, to hang out. Our society seems to work against finding connections, against developing and nurturing relationships over time. Instead of linking people together, the Internet's great worldwide web actually can create the opposite— islands of individuals talking to other isolated individuals without any personal contact. We are a people struggling to find community amidst the diversity in our world and the complexities of our scientific and technological advancements. How can we practice the art of hanging out? We become who we are through the relationships we develop over time. The sad commentary on our lives is that many have neither—relationships nor time.

I'd like to return to Mary Catherine Bateson for help in finding an alternative vision for how we find community in our crazy world. She has spent a lifetime living in multiple contexts. As the daughter of Margaret Mead and Gregory Bateson, she traveled all over the world. As an adult, she has made many different places home for herself and her family. Much of her writing struggles with themes of adapting to new places, living in diverse cultures, finding ways to navigate complex situations. Bateson uses metaphors of improvisation and multiple lenses for addressing her questions. Her questions are mine as well. How do we not only survive but live well in a complex, global, pluralistic world? Bateson's use of improvisation is not just a catchy idea for a trendy strategy. She uses it to offer a different way of addressing the diversity that many find threatening. Bateson's model emphasizes living and learning precisely through adapting to change and listening to the past. Improvisation occurs through the relationships that develop through time and care. She states:

> The basic challenge we face today in an interdependent world is to disconnect the notion of difference from the notion of superiority, to turn the unfamiliar into a resource rather than a threat. We know we can live with difference—men and women for instance have lived together throughout history. We know we can benefit from difference. But the old equation of difference with inferiority keeps coming back, as fatal to the effort to work together to solve the world's problems as the idea of competing for a limited good.[2]

We face multiple options for our lives; heterogeneousness surrounds us. We can go on playing our parts, content to just read the music. Or we can listen to the new strains of music around us, wondering how we might fit into the new sounds. Listening to the new requires attention to the old. As we compose our own music, we must listen to what has gone before us. Bateson explains:

> From the point of view of composing a life or managing an institution, the ability to recognize any situation as representing both continuity and change makes it possible to play that double recognition in tune with changing needs, to avoid the changes that reduce flexibility and the constancies that eat away at the necessities of survival.[3]

We know that willingness to change and to adapt to life's contingencies requires a certain kind of support from others. It is much more difficult to face what is new if we cut ourselves off from the support of others. The way we live determines with whom we live. How we are related to others determines who we are. We are who we are with others.

We are created in the image of God as creatures made for relationship. Similar to Bateson's ideas, the musical model of improvisation helps to explain God's presence and action in our world, invites reflection on the relationship between God and the world, and offers a model for how to find community in a diverse world. Human communities are constructed from relationships both within the human world and within the world of nature. The model of improvisation values the context of an interdependent community in which power is shared and the music depends on the interplay of chance and law, freedom and constraint, individuals and groups. There is no universal form of community; communities rise from their contextual settings. "Almost everywhere, however, a person is one who knows more others even as she or he is known: more than living tissue, a participant."[4] We are known by the company we keep. We participate in the construction of our identities by our relationships with nature, with our selves, with others, and, most importantly, with God. But what kind of relationships? How do we best live with one another?

Improvisation: A Theological Model for God and the World

The way we know ourselves as human community has often defined our theological understanding of the God/world relationship as a community. Scripture and tradition offer multiple metaphors for describing the human/divine relationship. Some have been more constructive than others have, as some have served to destroy human connectedness. For example, models of monarchical power, which portray God as king and the world as the kingdom, do not seem adequate for explaining how it is that God is present in our current world. This model has been used to emphasize patriarchal, hierarchical relationships. These relational dynamics correspond to the context in which we try to set the problem of divine agency and presence. We must find other models that offer an alternative vision of what it means to be in relationship with one another and with God. Our experience tells us that we have a sense of freedom, within certain constraints, and that God is both creator and redeemer of our world. These dimensions form the boundaries for sorting through the complexities of divine agency.

We need a new model that is both adequate for the Christian world and contextually meaningful for our scientific and pluralistic world. New discussions between theology and science offer complex conversations about God's agency in the quantum realm. Although these discussions are integral and important, they will not mean much to many people whose knowledge of quantum physics is negligible. These discussions must relate to other metaphors in our lives or they will have no relevance, or relevance to only a few scholars. The ethical questions about our world cannot be absent from these discussions. We must ask how God is active in ways that are consonant with modern science but that also fit with our human, social experience. This is the point at which I believe aesthetic or artistic models function well. They develop from contemporary culture and serve both to model and to critique current social structures. Not every model is useful. I follow the lead of theologian-scientists such as Arthur Peacocke, who draw on the image of composer/composition to link the insights of modern science with the claims of the Christian tradition.

Peacocke is best known for his use of musical models to describe God's interaction with the world. It is his work that inspired my further reflection on the images of jazz and blues. His model is tied to his understanding of *creatio continua,* of the ongoing nature of God's creation of the world. The artistic, aesthetic model lifts up the juxtapositions of creator/creature, freedom/constraint, law/chance. Humans display a sense of freedom that must be taken into account in this model. Peacocke settles on the metaphor of music as one that occurs as a "common theme both in classical (Greek and Roman) and the biblical literature of creation by God being the formation of order, a 'cosmos,' out of 'chaos.'"[5] Peacocke relates this musical model to themes in science of the processes of the natural world. God is understood to be the Great Improviser. Peacocke explains:

Thus might the Creator be imagined to enable to be unfolded the potentialities of the universe which he himself has given it, nurturing by his redemptive and providential actions those that are to come to fruition in the community of free beings— an Improviser of unsurpassed ingenuity.[6]

Peacocke relates the improvisation of Bach to this image of the Creator. Then he picks up on the notion of jazz as a more contemporary model for improvisation:

Or perhaps a more modern model for those of other tastes might be the extemporization of a jazz virtuoso, say, in Preservation Hall in New Orleans. Introduction of improvisation into this model of God as composer incorporates that element of open adaptability which any model of God's relation to a partly non-deterministic world should, however inadequately, represent.[7]

The advantages to Peacocke's model are numerous. Music is a social experience to which most humans can relate. The model of improvisation also fits with the new discoveries being made in the sciences.

Our theological models must consider our vastly diverse, rapidly changing world described by the contemporary sciences of evolutionary biology, quantum physics, and complexity. The new sciences describe in macro and micro ways how our world works. They describe both the human and nonhuman worlds. In a wonderful piece of literary journalism, Mitchell Waldrop describes the new science of complexity:

Instead of being a quest for the ultimate principles, it would be about flux, change, and the forming and dissolving of patterns. Instead of ignoring everything that wasn't uniform and predictable, it would have a place for individuality and the accidents of history. Instead of being about simplicity, it would be about—well, complexity.[8]

The models we use to describe the world must allow for its complexity and unpredictability. Relationships adapt through fluidity, elasticity, and the passage of time. Freedom and spontaneity are as characteristic of the world as order and structure. The metaphor of jazz is about improvising in a changing world, about the forming and dissolving of complex patterns.

Our evolutionary history tells the story of our physical makeup and of our social relationships. Order emerges through the complex building of relationships. Communities, whether cells or human social systems, reflect this evolutionary history. Waldrop's chronicle of the Santa Fe Institute tells the story of the creative process of science. Because the Newtonian model of life as a simple, organized machine doesn't seem to fit all of life, the new science of complexity describes the world as unpredictable, chaotic, and novel. Waldrop notes,

> What really galvanized him was the realization that here was a messy world—the interior of a living cell—that was at least as complicated as the messy human world. One tiny accident can change everything. Life develops. It has a *history.* Maybe, he thought, maybe that's why this biological world seems so spontaneous, organic, and—well, alive.[9]

The internal structure of a cell reflects the patterning of life in human social systems. All life is interwoven, exhibiting spontaneity, organism, and energy. Many of these same patterns can be found in the behaviors of the jazz community.

Paul F. Berliner's rich study of the jazz community includes a chapter entitled "Hangin' Out and Jammin': The Jazz Community as an Educational System."[10] With great detail, he describes the process of learning how to improvise within the jazz community. Much like my mother's senior friends, jazz musicians have perfected the art of hanging out in the jam session. During these informal sessions great learning takes place. Individuals share their talents by forming casual apprenticeships. Jam sessions bring together amateurs and professionals to learn from and with one another. The jam session creates its own community for learning how to improvise.

These communities developed in the jam session extend to the relationships developed over periods of time between teacher and student. Learning occurs through mentoring. Berliner comments, "With respect to the technical aspects of jazz, mentors typically create a congenial atmosphere for learning by conveying the view that student and teacher alike are involved in an ongoing process of artistic development and that the exchange of knowledge is a mutual affair."[11] One-on-one friendships nurtured over years are the "schools" for many jazz musicians. These friendships extend into the larger arenas of performers' homes and times at the clubs where informal playing can go on for long hours. Jam sessions set the musicians free to take risks. Diverse cross sections of people come together to just play and learn from one another. The jam session remains an open system where diverse people with diverse talents can come together to learn.

These rich, multifaceted, multileveled communities encourage and foster the individual expression of each player. Learning occurs individually through the support of the jazz community. "Overall, the jazz community's educational system sets the students on paths of development directly related to their goal: the creation of a unique improvisational voice within the jazz tradition."[12] The jazz community exemplifies the constant struggle between leadership and following, interdependence and individual freedom. The goal of a jazz community is to find the balance where the individual's freedom to improvise is grounded in the support of the ensemble. The individual plays freely but within the group. Limits are set for the dynamic of freedom.

Max DePree's quote at the beginning of this chapter lifts up this image of musical servanthood as a model for how a jazz group functions: "A jazz band is an expression of servant leadership. The leader of a jazz band has the beautiful opportunity to draw out the best of other musicians."[13] In this picture, the group lends its support as each member learns to discover her or his own musical voice. This image of servanthood is hardly one of master/slave, but one where power is shared and nurtured among all the members of the group. Leadership is not dominance, but empowerment.

The model of jazz as community offers alternative forms of community in contrast to the standard models in music. As we noted in chapter 1, much of Euro-Western music has been defined by the model of a symphony, in which the director is the main force and the players read their music. Although there is much interplay in classical music between the orchestra/director/ audience, the model of jazz accentuates different elements and emphasizes interdependence among all three in a freer manner.

In fact, jazz has often functioned as a social alternative to mainstream culture. In particular, the culture of bebop served as a critique of mainstream jazz and other culturally sanctioned forms of music. Bebop, developed from 1939 to 1941, served as an alternative to the big-band swing music of the predominantly white corporate culture.

> Compared to the swing jazz from which it grew, bebop was a conversational music, played best in small ensembles rather than in big bands. Intersubjective reality was manifested in the way the music emerged, as each player maintained a spontaneous awareness of voices within and without. Bebop innovators also worked to integrate mind and body by exploring the realm of prosody: that boundary between ideas and feelings where music becomes an utterance, and words become pure sound...Bebop represented a healthy separatism and autonomy on the part of black culture, after the commercialized assimilationism of swing.[14]

Bebop was an improvisational movement that served as a cultural critique. Working closely together in small groups, the musicians supported one another's growth and experimentation. They also extended the musical language, both tonally and rhythmically. The harmonious consonances from which so much music developed were challenged by the dissonances of extended chords, which often ended the piece. Tonic resolution was not always desirable. As well, the rhythms became embodied patterns for their own expression. The authority of the group was in the members instead of the fixed authority of the conductor. All these challenged the traditional "white" pattern of playing jazz. Consequently, bebop "embodied a more radical cultural stance than European modernist music, because it provided a more democratic and participatory form of musical expression."[15] As bebop functioned to critique white Western music, especially white swing, we might learn from this jazz idiom in order to further develop the model for theological constructions. How can we adapt this language of jazz and bebop to the theological language of divine action? Improvisation may be the task at hand.

God's Action in the World

The problem of divine agency continues to perplex us. Even our language troubles us when we try to explain how God acts in our world. Lurking behind the problem of divine agency are the issues of God's omnipotence and goodness, and the problem of evil. How can we explain God's action in the world? To do so, we must have some understanding of the world in which we live. God's action is not only in human affairs but also in the whole of the created order. We understand this domain of our life to be explained by the natural sciences. Humans are biosocial, cultural animals that require technical scientific explanations for our behavior. If this is the world in which we live, we must surely relate our understanding of God to it.

The Christian tradition has used many different models to explain how God is present in our world and works in creation. Sallie McFague's work on theological models summarizes the way they function.[16] McFague's work, along with that of other feminist and liberation scholars, is important for the work of theological models and the specific issue of divine agency. McFague always contextualizes her conceptual issues within the framework of the world situation. Her early work discussed the role of God in a nuclear age, and her current work suggests that theology must address the environmental/ecological crisis. Theology is more than mere response to the current crisis of the age; it must also respond to and shape tradition. McFague has tried to meet that challenge. She claims that some models work better than others do. For example, during the scientific revolution and the Age of Enlightenment, the model of universe as machine functioned to explain the world and God's relationship to it. Deism results from this picture. However, we tend to favor certain pictures, such as this monarchical picture, over others. In fact, we idolize them, turning them into our gods. Like the Israelites in Exodus, we construct our gods in silver and gold to protect ourselves from facing what we don't want to see. McFague's critique of certain models highlights their irrelevant and idolatrous nature. She calls theologians to the task of constructing or reconstructing models that fit our world:

> Metaphorical theology is a post-modern, highly skeptical, heuristic enterprise, which claims that in order to be faithful to the God of its tradition—the God on the side of life and its fulfillment—we must try out new pictures that will bring the reality of God's love into the imaginations of the women and men of today.[17]

McFague's theological work is committed to exploring new metaphorical language and models for theological language. Her task is ours as well: "The question we must ask is not whether one is true or the other false, but which one is a better portrait of Christian faith *for our day*."[18] Our theological models can never somehow approximate reality, especially divine reality. Models serve to spur the imagination, to lure one into new ways of thinking, and to find ways of making the divine agency of God come alive in our postmodern world. If particular models are interesting, that is, if they are fruitful for further provocations, they are more likely truer to our experience than other models.

The theological tradition has often used spatial and temporal language to explain God's presence and action in the world. Very often theological models are tied to the social-scientific frameworks of the age. Those models change slowly. We use many of the models from the past to talk today about God's relationship to the world. Some models emphasize the human realm as the arena of God's grace, while others emphasize the natural world as if God is absent from human affairs. Deism is an example of the latter. However, deism must be flatly rejected as a Christian model of divine agency. Christian theology claims that God is near and present in our world. On the other hand, Christian theology has veered too far when it claims that everything is God's will, without any distinctions made. Here God ends up as a dictator who sanctions atrocities such as the Holocaust.

Scripture and Christian tradition can be reexamined for biblical images that respond to our world and are faithful in their roots. For example, the playful images of Sophia, of Johannine eucharistic language, First Peter's language of the household of faith, and Pauline images of the body of Christ provide rich resources for reexamining biblical language. These models emphasize the communal, interrelated character of the God/world relationship. The creation of God is a celebration of relationships. Joseph Sittler explains, "Just as God placed his creature, man, in a garden and commanded him to 'tend' it, so the world of nature—God's other creation—is spoken of as man's context in which is celebrated the orchestration of relatedness."[19]

The model of improvisation in a jazz band or blues group highlights ways in which we can re-image God's presence and action in our world. Many feminist theologians and process theologians have used the image of the world as God's body. This fits well with ecological concerns and emphasizing the immanence of God. However, I have argued elsewhere, and agree with Ian Barbour, that this model of "the cosmic organism does not allow sufficiently for the freedom either of God or of human agents in relation to each other. It also has difficulty in adequately representing God's transcendence."[20] Barbour relies on the model provided by process theologians, among others.

The process model correlates with the themes of a model of improvisation, of co-creatorship. God functions as a "creative participant" in the community, but God also provides the matrix for creativity and the structures of the way the world works. In this model, God is truly categorically different, but God is also transcendent because of the relatedness with creation.[21] This works not only with improvisation but also with a scientific worldview. Barbour explains, "Process thought is consonant with an ecological and evolutionary understanding of nature as a dynamic and open system, characterized by emergent levels of organization, activity, and experience."[22] The order of the community is contextually discovered by the participants. This emphasis on community is also consonant with another of Barbour's models, the *kenotic model.* This model explains God's self-limitation of omnipotence to allow reciprocity and vulnerability in relationship to the rest of creation. Here one calls to mind the kenotic passage in Paul's letter to the Philippians (2:5–7). Barbour notes that this accords with analogies of "artistic creativity and parental love."[23]

This model views God as the ground or matrix of creativity from which improvisation and novelty flow. God works cooperatively with creatures to inspire their work in creation.

The relationship between God and the creature is contextually dependent. Also, this model of musical improvisation is an expression of servant leadership, in which the leader of the community empowers others in the group and does not dominate the composition.

The relationship between God and the world is a living, dynamic relationship. Such a relationship is established, renewed, and recreated through the world's encounter with the Triune God. Joseph Sittler notes:

> He [Jesus] speaks, rather, of God and of man and of the human community in a relational and living fashion, and on the way, in the course of his speech swoops down, now here, now there; picks up some detail, situation, instance of human pathos, error, pride, holds it up for a moment, and then moves on.[24]

God moves in and through creation like a bird on the wing. The way God works in the world is never forced or captured, but God moves like the breath of the wind. With this model providing a new framework from which to explore the issue of divine power and creaturely freedom, God becomes the great improviser, the one nurturing our parts in the music. God relates to the world like a musician to the audience, like a soloist to the band, like a conductor to the group.

In this model, God works within and inside creation, not merely as some external force that works from "above" or from "without" creation. God works spontaneously in and through the experience of each creature sensitive to the environment. Joseph Bracken uses such images to talk about God's work in the world:

> Thus, within this scheme God and the creature endowed with subjectivity mutually condition and affect one another. In that sense, God does indeed take risks with creatures since God cannot predetermine how the creature will respond to the divine initial aim. But, on the other hand, the creature is clearly endowed with spontaneity. There is no question about its "free" decision being incorporated into a world order which is already chosen in its entirety by God. The world order within this scheme is still unfolding even for God. That is, even God cannot

know with certitude what the creature will choose until after the creature chooses it. God, in other words, just adjusts to what creatures decide and thus inevitably takes risk in dealing with creatures.[25]

Bracken raises the difficult questions about God's foreknowledge and power. If creatures really are free to create and improvise, how does this relate to the traditional notions of omniscience and omnipotence?

God's role is multifaceted in this model, providing both leadership and support for the ensemble. The contrast to the classical symphony orchestra conductor is noteworthy. The image of conductor changes, as does the music. Mary Catherine Bateson explains, "Jazz exemplifies artistic activity that is at once individual and communal, performance that is both repetitive and innovative, each participant sometimes providing background support and sometimes flying free."[26] God gives order and yet is the ground from which comes creativity and novelty. God is also the playful dancer, the Wisdom of the World. God's leadership, like the jazz bandleader's, will encourage each member to find his or her own musical voice. The music occurs within the nurturing atmosphere where each individual can perfect the art of hanging out. Community occurs over time through the rich interactions of relationships, particularly between Creator and creation. Improvisation is interdependence set to rhythm. Now we can extend this composition to the community we call church.

Christian Identity as Interdependent Community

Christian identity is always relational—to self, to God, and to creation. We know that Jesus promises to be present wherever two or three are gathered. The Holy Spirit is sent as Comforter, as Companion. God's relationship begins with the covenants established with the people of Israel and is extended into the body of Christ, the church. Joseph Sittler situated his early work on Christian ethics within the framework of community:

> God's covenant is with a people; one of Jesus' most impassioned statements of his mission is the word "gather"; and the obedience of primitive faith immediately understood its proper

form in terms of a community of "the called" to "membership" in a "fellowship" which is "the household of faith" and which is "his body, the church."[27]

When we worship, we use the invocation as the gathering of the people of God. We are named as God's people; we who were once "no people" are now "God's people.' Community forms the church and gives the believer an identity. But the community of God is first grounded in the doctrine of creation, in which all of life belongs and has its dependence on God. To be a Christian is, first and foremost, to receive one's identity as a creature.

Christian communities are an ambiguous mixture of institutionalized hierarchy and alternative models of shared leadership. Our history is mixed as we understand the way that we gather together as community. When Christianity became the institutionalized religion of the fourth-century Roman Empire, its original models of servant leadership vanished as Christianity adapted to the power structure of the Roman Empire. However, throughout the history of Christendom, varied reformers and groups offered alternative ways of being together. Monastic communities were created as an alternative to the papal hierarchy. Once at a meeting I spoke with another academic who taught at a Benedictine college in Illinois. He said that for most of the monks it was more important to be Benedictine than to be Catholic. This was my experience when I was on sabbatical at St. John's College in Collegeville, Minnesota, and as I visited with the community of sisters at St. Benedict's. The best way to be a good Catholic was to be a good Benedictine. That often meant, however, deviating from the patterns of the Roman Catholic hierarchy. An example was the letter written in a journal by some of the monks, offering public support for the ordination of women. These acts of leadership created alternative ways of seeing and experiencing community.

Larry Rasmussen, a Lutheran ethicist, reminds us that the very act of shaping communities is as important as the community that is shaped. He likens the act of shaping communities to the choreography of dance. Dance, like jazz and other musical forms, requires both freedom and structure. He remarks,

Communities, in order to *be* communities, must be ordered, cared for, led. The other reason is equally vital: governance is necessary for the positive flourishing of life. Proper ordering, as any gardener, cook, orchestra conductor, or housekeeper can tell you, is basic to good living. Sheer randomness is not the highest state of being. Thriving, not to say surviving, requires the creative ordering of freedom.[28]

Rasmussen suggests that models of Christian leadership must be thought of as "creative deviance on the front line."[29] Christian communities, particularly those in which Jesus functioned, proposed an alternative form to the current hierarchy. Rasmussen labels the governance style of these communities as "community democracy," which includes or depends on "shifting leadership, high levels of member participation, the capacity of its organizers and troublemakers to see through the dominant ways of doing things, and a collective ability to offer alternatives."[30] This model of "community democracy" is similar to the model of improvisation in a blues or jazz group.

Rasmussen notes that the model of kingdom that Jesus preaches is radically different from those in the society. "His is an upside-down kingdom whose ways contrast with those of 'kings' and 'benefactors.' In his reign, he tells them, status distinctions are reversed."[31] Like the words of DePree about jazz, the community models of Jesus emphasize a servant leadership in which the model of power is one of egalitarianism. Or even more radically, Jesus lifts up to positions of power those whom society rejects as unworthy.

The model of jazz, like the models offered by Rasmussen, accents the church as a model of alternative community. Creative improvisation is a way of living together amidst ambiguity and uncertainty. Rasmussen notes that our time is like that of ancient Hellenism:

diverse, cosmopolitan, multilingual, multiracial, multicultural, multireligious, fragmented, eclectic, riddled by extremes of all kinds, and more than a little violent. We often feel dislocated and off-center, just as people did then. In the world of early Christianity, the solidity of empire was giving way, and new

configurations were in the making, many of them bedeviled
by chaos and confusion. Almost everyone worried about moral
degradation.[32]

Many different models must be adapted to diverse communities.
Not everyone will function well with the same model. Different
communities face different problems and must be allowed to
use their own resources to adapt, to solve, and to create new
ways of living. Rasmussen lists qualities that make for "community
democracy and creative deviance." All the qualities emphasize
a form of governance and leadership that goes against the grain
of a powerful hierarchy in which power is not shared. Rasmussen
notes that we must find multiple ways of experimenting with
leadership so that it emerges from "the foot and sides of the
table as well as the head. Innovation arises from the diversity of
members, just as unity issues from joint action."[33]

Creativity is a mark of a community that adapts to ambiguous,
chaotic situations. John Cobb's use of creation transformation
reinforces this creative element in the improvisational act.
Creativity is linked to improvisation in the works of both Cobb
and Robert Mesle. Cobb explains that the tradition itself needs
to be transformed:

> Furthermore, the process of transformation of the tradition is
> not subject merely to good will. It requires creative imagination
> and mutual support, extensive experimentation, and willingness
> to try again after failures. The theological task is demanding,
> but not obscure or irrelevant.[34]

Theology, like its subject matter, demands transformation. As
Cobb notes, the "creative transforming power of God" is incarnate
in Jesus the Christ. To experience creative transformation is to
be "in Christ." Faith is a living process in which the body of
Christ, the community of people, lives in creative tension with
the current culture and the tradition of the faith.

Martin Luther's notion of the priesthood of all believers fits
Rasmussen's notions of "community democracy and creative
deviance" and Cobb's image of Christ as creative transformation.
Philip Hefner translates Luther's concept of the priesthood of all
believers into his version, called the "people's church." He uses
this concept to critique the clericalism and elitism present in the

current Lutheran Church. Hefner says, "These considerations point to my working definition of the 'people's church': *The church life is intimately bound up in the actual realities of the lived-out lives of its people and the cultural expressions of these realities.*"[35] Church must be that which incarnates the lives and experiences of peoples in local communities. The notion of church is necessarily pluriform and multifarious, not for its own sake, but for the sake of God's incarnation in human possibilities. Therefore, no form of church can ever be considered final.

In moves similar to those of feminists and liberation theologians, Hefner calls for a transition from "one church," an official church, to a church that adapts to the lives and needs of "the people." The "people's church" functions as an alternative and critique to the abstract, elitist form of some "pure church." Hefner says,

> The more accurate image is that of a transition from a more mono-cultural official and elite church to what we call a church of "social polychromy," a polychrome whose official and elite character is rooted in the church of the peoples. The turmoil and discomfort will not disappear, but they will be understood as signals of a future happening quite differently from what our current discussion understands.[36]

Like the dissonance in music that is at first difficult to listen to, the rich notes of diversity are the harbinger of an adventurous and rich future for the church. However, we must learn to listen to these new sounds. The tendency with such diversity is to try and blend it into the rest of the composition in such a way that the dissonance doesn't bother *our* understanding of harmony.

Hefner makes an important point that diversity and unity are two poles of experience that must be kept in tension. One cannot exist without the other. If we listen to the new possibilities that God creates for us in church, are we ready to work with the new sounds and sights? Hefner comments on our perspective on diversity within communities:

> Our diversities do not exist chiefly as elements awaiting some kind of unification or harmonization in a more stable multicultural community. Rather, diversities constitute a symphony of identities whose possibilities undergo the

transformations that God's future requires. Rather than viewing our diversities through the lens of unity, we should see them as synergy, a working together. We should not be focusing as much attention on harmonizing or unifying our diversities as on listening to them, so that we can better understand our identities today as we attempt to respond in the present to God's call into the future that the Creator God has prepared for us.[37]

The celebration of diversity requires work and careful attention. If the church is going to be effective in this next century, it must pay attention to the culture and world in which it lives. We cannot live in some sort of splendid isolation or in fear of our culture. Instead, the culture presents to us questions about how we live as Christians in the world.

Community as Church

For Luther, church was both the hidden and visible community where the preaching of the gospel and the administration of the sacraments occurred, an event of God's people living out their commitments to God's word. Eric Gritsch and Robert Jenson comment, "The church is neither an invisible Platonic-reality—as some of the *Schwaemer* argued—nor an infallible, unchanging institution, as the papal church claimed."[38] Luther understood the church as a concrete, historical community active in the world on behalf of the neighbor. In other words, the church is not a place, but an event, not a product to be sold, but a process to be experienced. In fact, "Luther stressed the noninstitutional character of the church. He disliked the word 'church' (*Kirche*) and preferred terms such as 'assembly' (*Sammlung*) and 'community' (*Gemeinde*)."[39] The body of believers is a community shaped by its interaction with the Word of God, preached in kerygma of Jesus the Christ. Luther even referred to the church as an aural event; he called it a "mouth house" (*Mundhaus*).[40] The gospel of Jesus Christ is really the only "necessary mark of the church."[41] What mattered most to Luther was that God's unconditional promise of God's grace be active in the community re-forming the lives of those who believe.

Gritsch and Jenson suggest that what is so radical about Luther's notion of church is that it is not simply a collection of people, but that something happens to people as *laos tou theou.* They explain:

> Neither a class of persons nor a structure is the church; the church is an event. Thus the Lutheran Reformation had from the start an actualist understanding of the church: the church is something *going on* in the world.[42]

Thus, Luther's dynamic notion of the church is rooted in the particularity of the article of justification by grace, the article by which the church stands or falls. However, the question of Luther's revolutionary ideas at work in our world is up for grabs. Twenty years ago when Gritsch and Jenson wrote their book, they claimed:

> Most of us will accept the formula, but we are able to do so only because we have to use "justification" for the relatively trivial matter of excuse for past offense, and have made "faith" mean religiosity or sincerity. If, having reminded ourselves of the original meaning of the formula, we visit the churches, and ask if anything happens in them that could by this criterion be called "the gospel," we will have to answer. It is this chapter in which it must be explicitly said: *the church is now in at least as desperate need of reformation as it was in the sixteenth century, and by the very same criterion as then.*[43]

Over the last twenty years Lutherans have struggled to form a new ecclesiological structure: the Evangelical Lutheran Church in America. With the formation of any institution comes the requisite debates about the nature of the institution. We have been issued "calls to faithfulness" and invitations to "reform the church." Both sides of the ecclesiological juncture, while differing radically in their approach, do agree that the church needs reformation. And the discussion about this is not just the province of the professionals.

A conversation with students in class one night provoked extensive discussion about the nature of the church as community and what the purpose of the church should be. The discussion resulted from our reading of Cobb's book *Lay Theology.* Cobb says that for mainline churches to survive and even prosper, laypeople must not relinquish theology to the professional academics. Cobb calls for laypeople to take seriously their task to be theologians, that is, to commit to "intentional Christian thinking about important Christian matters."[44] Cobb insists that we are called to challenge the tradition, for "the tradition is not satisfactory as it stands."[45] He contrasts those who are generally satisfied with their beliefs and are content to "transmit and apply" the tradition with others who might see their role as adapting and reforming the tradition. But Cobb calls laypeople to an even more radical and challenging task, that of "transforming the tradition." The vocation of the Christian is to transform Christianity.

God is at work bringing about new things in the world. Cobb's notion of transformation is similar to the theme of our calling as improvisers and creators in the world. Cobb does not call for a complete rejection of past traditions but for the transformation of the old into the new. He explains:

> According to my understanding of Christian faith, a major vocation of the Christian is to transform Christianity. My Christian commitment is to this transformation. We will not transform Christianity once and for all and then have the transformed Christianity to which we can commit ourselves. It is in the transforming that I find the effective presence of the living God. My deepest commitment is to this process of creative transformation rather than to any one or its product.[46]

Transformation takes that which was old and makes it new. This is a call not only to individuals but also to the church. What kind of community is needed for Christianity to be transformed? This seems to be a radical question.

I found an answer in a place I would not have first conceived of as radical. I love liturgical music and am often disappointed by how poorly we sing and worship together on Sunday mornings. A couple of years ago, I attended worship at St. Benedict's Abbey in Saint Joseph, Minnesota. This community of women worships several times a day and has been together as a community for decades. As my family and I listened to the liturgy and music, it struck us that something seemed unusual about this experience. I had a difficult time explaining to others why I found this to be such special and uplifting worship. Then days later I realized that I was not just one individual with other individuals, but that I had been asked to join a community of women whose identity is shaped by the singing of psalms, the reading of scripture, the breaking of bread. Of special interest to me was the amazing sound of the choir. They were not extremely gifted musicians, but they sounded different to me. Again, I realized that they sang not as a group who gather now and then but as an ensemble whose musical identity is shaped by deep community commitments. How different from most Sunday morning services, where most of us may know each other but do not hold that kind of history and continuity together. The witness of these Benedictine sisters for me was that they provided an alternative vision of worship in community, giving voice to a shape of life that celebrates the interdependence of each person. This notion of church is one that is often foreign to my experience. I realize that for many people this kind of commitment cannot be realized, but we can learn from how the Benedictine way of life witnesses to the rest of the world the nature of life together. They had developed community as a place of "hangin' out and jammin'."

Dietrich Bonhoeffer, in his little book *Life Together,* shares a similar vision of what radical community can offer to us. He notes that community is the relationship of the individuals within the community. These Benedictine women understand and exemplify his ideal of community:

> Not what a man is in himself as a Christian, his spirituality and piety, constitutes the basis of our community. What determines our brotherhood is what that man is by reason of Christ. Our community with one another consists solely in what Christ has done for us.[47]

The community in which Bonhoeffer lived helped him to survive in a deeply troubled, chaotic world. Not unlike many in our own world, Bonhoeffer faced struggles about how to live a Christlike life in community with others. His way of living is one that calls the Christian deeply into that world and not from the world. Like the Benedictine Sisters, Bonhoeffer offers an alternative vision of living amidst trouble and uncertainty. Christians are called into the world as a community. The community we call the church is a living organism that adapts to and with the world in which it exists. Both Bonhoeffer and the Benedictines offer their lives as witness within the Christian community to the world.

Some Christians find it tempting to use "the community" as a means of protection from the evils of the "world." The community of the church is often narrowly defined with boundaries to exclude those who are threatening, who are different, and who live on the margins of life. Very often these boundaries are not drawn explicitly, but we see the way they work implicitly in our congregational life on Sunday mornings. Recently, I listened to our pastor preach on Luke 14, where God challenges us to give a banquet and invite those who are blind, sick, lame, and unwanted. Our pastor challenged us to see the text not as some "moral requirement" but as a vision of how God treats and invites all of us. This vision of community functions to challenge our own narrow boundaries. She asked us to look around and really question whether our congregation had "welcomed the stranger." It's more comfortable to be with those who are similar, yet we know the world is not that way. We live in a world in which diversity marks our everyday experiences. How might the church respond to this challenge? Pastor Lehr's sermon corresponds to my thoughts on Bateson's imagery of peripheral vision and improvisation. Both challenge our "limited vision" and try to open new vistas and ways of seeing our life as a community in this world.

To be radical in this world might be to perfect the "art of hangin' out and jammin'." Berliner notes that it is musicians' "abiding devotion to the music that binds this diverse population together."[48] The jam session cuts across gender, race, age, and class to bind people together for the love of music. Paul tells us in Philippians to be of the same mind in Christ Jesus, "having the same love, being in full accord and of one mind. Do nothing from selfish ambition or conceit, but in humility regard others as better than yourselves" (2:2–3). Paul does not speak about a humility that gives self over to others with no regard, but encourages the self through love to be of the same mind with others in Christ. Paul's famous kenotic hymn that follows this passage might be the same kind of improvisational work that the Benedictines can teach us about how to perfect the art of hanging out in the world. As we find Christ together, we might be like those in a jam session, who can find an "abiding devotion to the music that binds," which will bind us together as the body of Christ.

WE ARE a people struggling to find community amidst the diversity in our world and the complexities of our scientific and technological advancements. How can we not only survive but live well in this world? We can practice the art of "hanging out." We become who we are through the relationships we develop over time.

4

THE BLUES:
AN AFFIRMATION THAT
LIFE STILL SWINGS

It's an attitude of affirmation in the face of difficulty, of improvisation in the face of challenge. It means you acknowledge that life is a low-down dirty shame yet confront that fact with perseverance, with humor, and above all, with elegance.

ALBERT MURRAY[1]

The old canard about the blues being "depressing" (or sexist, or simplistic) is a gross oversimplification. The blues celebrate the human condition in all its flawed beauty. They neither judge nor pontificate; rather they embrace contradiction, even at its most tormenting, as the essence and spice of life.

DAVID WHITEIS[2]

FEMINIST and liberation theologians offer a clue for listening to different kinds of music when they encourage us to listen to those whose experience begins in Lent, in suffering and pain. In the music of the blues, I hear voices that know the

85

depths of suffering and evil but that confront that evil with resistance and grace.

Lent

Lent is a problem. As a child, I never liked the season of Lent, the season from winter to spring, a season of burying the alleluia, of giving up favorite things, of snow changing to mud, of flowers not yet bloomed. I dreaded the long forty days that focused on death and pain and wondered why God allowed the death of his Son. Later, in college, I read theologians who said that Jesus' death was necessary either to pay the price of sin or to appease God's wrath. I was told in sermons and in the lessons from scripture that Christians were to take up their crosses and follow Jesus. I was never sure what that meant, but it was clear that Jesus' end was not one I wanted to face. Would suffering make me a good Christian? I wasn't sure I wanted to find out in reality, so I read novels about the martyrs (*Quo Vadis* and *The Robe*) and watched *Ben Hur.*

Lent meant sacrifice. I sang hymns with words such as these: "Glory be to Jesus, who in bitter pain, poured for me the life blood, from his sacred veins."[3] As a Lutheran, I often felt guilty that I didn't give up meat on Fridays and go to mass all the time like my Catholic friends. I'm still not sure now, years later, that I like Lent. But that is probably beside the point. I still have some of the same questions, but now they are even more poignant. In the face of the unbelievable suffering and evil in the world, I wonder where the cross has led Christians. The meaning of Jesus' life and death on the cross and the problem of evil interlock with each other in Christian theology. In theological categories, the doctrine of atonement is the category for interpreting the meaning of Jesus' life and death in response to the problem of suffering and evil. This doctrine alone has caused me great theological grief. I remember the first few times that I shared those concerns with other women and found that I was not alone. They didn't like Lent either.

Darby Kathleen Ray, in her book *Deceiving the Devil*, addresses the issues of atonement, abuse, and ransom from a feminist perspective. She continues the work already begun by many feminists and liberationists. Ray rightly notes that the church has never had an official doctrine of the atonement; interpretations vary as widely as human experience. Ray claims that Christianity offers two main explanations for how the life and death of Jesus confront and resist evil:

> In one line of thinking, Christ's death on the cross atones for human sin because he substitutes for or represents the sinner (substitutionary atonement). In another, Jesus' life and ministry offer a radically new alternative for living without sin (moral influence).[4]

Feminists are concerned that these atonement theories legitimize and sanction violence and abuse toward women and others who are vulnerable. Ray also notes that "liberationists are concerned that they [atonement theories] undermine human efforts to combat injustice and oppression by encouraging ethical passivity."[5] Both theories of the atonement are problematic; both need revision in light of feminist and liberationist critiques.

Part of the problem with atonement theories is that they often function in abstraction. Theologians, like me, are often guilty of creating elaborate theoretical abstractions that don't touch the ground of believers' experiences. Many Christians are unaware of the Anselmian and Abelardian atonement models, or of Aulen's model of *christus victor*. Most Christians understand and experience the meaning of Jesus' death from the hymns they sing, the sermons they hear, the creeds they profess, the scriptures they study, and the liturgies they use every week. Even these manifestations of Christian worship and life can function like the theoretical atonement theories of the experts. Neither reach the experiences of those whose lives have been battered and abused by the church. Christian theologians and practicing Christians must realize that the way we talk about the meaning of Jesus' death has been used to sanction (make holy) horrible violence and suffering. Witness events such as the Inquisition, slavery, the Holocaust, and domestic abuse. We cannot simply carry on theological business as usual.

Lent and the Passion of Christ are liturgical reminders to those who have suffered of how problematic the meaning of

Christ's life and death is for many people both within and outside the Christian faith. To Christians, the cross of Christ has been both a sign of resistance to evil and a symbol that has encouraged and glorified suffering. The doctrine of atonement creates theological and existential problems when the cross is used by those in power to glorify passivity and suffering. Abuse, slavery, and much suffering were caused by despotic Christian rulers and the god they had fashioned in their own image.

As a rather privileged, middle-class white woman, I am part of a Christian culture that has benefited from the suffering of others. As a woman, I have experienced and listened to the experiences of other women who have been oppressed and abused by leaders in the church. I decided a few years ago that my Lenten discipline is to ask the questions, to raise the difficult issues. To do so I must listen to others for the answers, listen to those who have suffered. What do those voices who have endured suffering and pain have to say about the cross and resurrection? What is the relationship of suffering to the Christian faith? Of the cross to the resurrection? Is Lent a "dead-end" season, or do we really believe it leads to the hope of the resurrection? Lent has come to be an in-between time for me. A time to be in-between seasons of winter and spring, a time to listen to transitions, a time of paying attention to the voices who know about pain and suffering. What do their voices tell me? What have I learned from listening to others and to myself?

Feminist and liberation theologians raise crucial insights and critiques about the doctrine of atonement. However, many Christians are threatened by these voices because they take issue with the heart of the Christian faith. Such Christians ask, How can one possibly question the meaning of the cross of Christ and still be a good Christian? However, feminists also ask the question, How can one remain a Christian if the central symbol of the faith has been used to persecute and even sanction the abuse and torture of those whom the church has labeled as "other," as dangerous? This question must be faced with courage. Sometimes the options seem limited. I could ignore the painful questions and go about my business as usual, or I could abandon Christianity altogether. But another option exists that I believe holds possibility. I could listen to new voices, to new sounds that have alternative ways of critiquing and interpreting the central message of Christianity.

Who are these voices? Feminist and liberation theologians offer a clue for listening to different kinds of music when they encourage us to listen to those whose experience *begins* in Lent, in suffering and pain. Robert McAfee Brown tells white, North American Christians that if Easter is to have meaning, we must listen to the voices that know about the experience of sin, death, and evil. In an early work, *Theology in a New Key: Responding to Liberation Themes,* Brown listens to the voices of liberation theologians to reinterpret the "harmonies" of the Christian faith.[6] Many voices have not been allowed to sing their own songs, or when they do, Christians have labeled them as "other," as "demonic." Brown notes,

> Many terms have been used to describe these articulators of the theology in a new key—the "wretched of the earth," the poor, the oppressed, the marginalized, the voiceless, the exploited, the victims. Their spokespersons vary and their agendas vary...The most condescending thing possible would be to try to group them, or lump them or generalize about them. But they have at least this in common: *they have been denied a voice and have been without hope; they now demand a voice and that gives them hope.*[7]

The music of such voices is sung from the experience of life, *not* in theological abstractions or theories. Life itself is the text; voices of pain and suffering are the melodies. Diverse voices give shape to the structure of the compositions. Brown's argument calls for a new way of listening, of paying attention to the new compositions. "Just as a composer may prepare the way in which the diminished seventh will be resolved, so the history of recent theology may prepare us for the new directions, so that we will neither reject them as outrageous nor be so surprised by them that we fail to take them seriously."[8]

Instead of beginning in the church or with other theologians, I want to step outside and listen to those who play and sing the music in different places. I love all kinds of music, but lately I have found the blues and jazz to be voices that reach me in new and different ways. In the music of the blues, I hear voices that know the depths of suffering and evil but that confront that evil with resistance and with grace. Ironically, the blues have often been labeled as music of the devil. It might be that this "bedevilment" of tradition will lead to its transformation. Albert Murray's work, and that of other blues and jazz theorists on the image of the "blues idiom" and "blues hero," connects to themes that I find present in feminist and liberation theology. The purpose of this chapter is to listen carefully to the voices of those who sing the blues both in music and in theology in order to re-vision the doctrine of atonement so that it is not used to legitimize suffering and perpetuate evil. I hope to offer ways for subverting and recreating the traditional doctrine of atonement, for listening to theology in a new key. We need music not only in new keys but in new genres.

Listening to the Music: "Sonny's Blues"

> Then Creole stepped forward to remind them that what they were playing was the blues. He hit something in all of them, he hit something in me, myself, and the music tightened and deepened, apprehension began to beat the air. Creole began to tell us what the blues were all about. They were not about anything very new. He and his boys up there were keeping it new, at the risk of ruin, destruction, madness, and death, in order to find new ways to make us listen.[9]

"Sonny's Blues," told by James Baldwin, creates a universal hero who, through the power of his music, transforms his life and the lives of those around him. James Cone, an African American theorist and theologian, explains that "the blues are a transformation of black life through the sheer power of song."[10] The blues create heroes who rise above their misery and suffering as they transform their lives through the experience of the music. The story of the universal hero of the blues is told poignantly in this particular tale. Baldwin has been called one of the most important writers of twentieth-century America. Tutored under Richard Wright, Baldwin developed his own style as a novelist (*Go Tell It on the Mountain*) and as an essayist.

Baldwin draws the reader into the world of Harlem. He orchestrates the composition that tells of two brothers who work out their individual callings in life amidst the poverty and racial tensions of the New York City setting. Following the tradition of the blues, the story builds and weaves its theme through the laments and songs of many different voices. Baldwin captures his audience with the indigos and pale blue tones of the jazz and blues genre of African American literature. The story's truth is in the playing. "The blues are true because they combine art and life, poetry and experience, the symbolic and the real. They are an artistic response to the chaos of life. And to sing the blues truthfully, it is necessary to experience the historical realities that created them."[11] "Sonny's Blues" combines the setting of Harlem with the poetry of the music. Baldwin offers his readers a way to move through the chaos of life to a new way of being whole in the world, of playing one's own music.

The story opens with Sonny's brother, a high school teacher, struggling with his fears about Sonny's release from prison. Like so many of the students his brother sees every day, Sonny had become imprisoned by drugs. Fearful that Sonny will never really escape the bondage of prison and addiction, his brother receives a note from Sonny saying that he will soon be released. His time is done. "I didn't want to believe that I'd ever see my brother going down, coming to nothing, all that light in his face gone out, in the condition I'd already seen so many others."[12] Not having seen Sonny for more than a year, his brother is shocked when Sonny comes home to see that he is "older and thinner" and that the time in prison "had deepened the distant stillness in which he had always moved."[13]

When Sonny was younger, he had wanted to be a jazz musician, to play *with* jazz musicians. He admired Charlie Parker, the greatest musician in his eyes. Sonny's piano was his reason for living, for rising above the conditions of his life that seemed to entrap him. He returns home from prison to live with his brother, and one day they find themselves watching a revival meeting and listening to the gospel music. What follows is a poignant discussion about the nature of suffering. At the end of their discussion, Sonny comments while looking out the window, "All that hatred down there…all that hatred and misery and love. It's a wonder it doesn't blow the avenue apart."[14]

That night they go together to a nightclub, to a place jam-packed, dark, and noisy. Moving from one family to another, Sonny takes his brother into the club, where he joins in a group to play the blues. Creole and the other musicians in the group welcome Sonny into their musical family. This is Sonny's world. The atmosphere changes, and the "lights on the bandstand, on the quartet, turned to a kind of indigo."[15]

Sonny's brother explains that when most of us hear music, we really don't "listen." Even if we do, most of the music enters into us as personal. "But the man who creates the music is hearing something else, is dealing with the roar rising from the void and imposing order on it as it hits the air."[16] The musicians begin and call Sonny into the dialogue. During the first set of music in the nightclub, Sonny isn't moved to the depths, yet he knows the waters. Slowly, the conversation develops again, and Sonny enters into the "deep water." Moving into the waters of the music, Creole accompanies Sonny into the blues, transforming the watery chaos into order. "He was Sonny's witness that deep water and drowning were not the same thing—he had been there, and he knew. And he wanted to know. He was waiting for Sonny to do the things on the keys which would let Creole know that Sonny was in the water."[17] Sonny's improvisation is idiomatic; it's his own scales and tune. He has waded into the deep blue waters and can swim. He will not drown this time.[18] As in a baptism, Sonny's genesis begins.

The blues tell the story of how we suffer, but there is more. "For, while the tale of how we suffer, and how we are delighted, and how we may triumph is never new, it always must be heard. There isn't any other tale to tell, it's the only light we've got in all this darkness."[19] Sonny's music frees others. To listen is to be free. The music has led him through the waters of chaos to the new life of freedom and hope. Soaking wet, standing in the indigo light, Sonny has changed not only himself but also those who have listened to his music. His blues become the music of freedom.

Baldwin composes a story of the transformation of people who want to find freedom in their own story, in their own music. Part of this transformation occurs through the changes of the musical forms. Sonny is shaped by the music of Charlie Parker and other bebop artists. Sonny's music takes the form of these new voices, shapes the notes, and comments on the old blues and jazz. In a commentary on "Sonny's Blues," Tracey Sherard notes that "the 'blues' Sonny plays are a commentary on the historical context and function of the blues Baldwin suggests are inadequate to convey the 'sad stories' of urban Harlem."[20] Baldwin is not critiquing the blues itself, but

> advocating the necessity of African Americans' self-awareness of the context of their own cultural forms, and particularly of the hybrid narratives that can result from their appropriation...Jazz, I argue, represents a revision of the blues that allows for commentary on the disappointing economic and social conditions of African American urban culture—in "Sonny's Blues," specifically, the conditions of Harlem's Ghetto.[21]

Sonny's blues are not the laments of victims caught by "disappointing economic and social conditions." Sonny's blues transfigure the cultural laments into a new form of music, with new shapes and sounds. Bebop revolted against the music of the dominant white culture, particularly swing. In this story, bebop is a cultural commentary on the old and a metaphor for creating new ways of being in the world. Creole's dialogue with Sonny allows Sonny to move where he has been afraid to go. The old way is familiar, with all its pitfalls and familiar traps. The new way beckons; Sonny follows with courage and hope.

Sonny's music is also different from the gospel sounds he and his brother listened to earlier in the story at the revival meeting. The old forms of music were being challenged with new sounds, new voices, new ways of being in the world. Sherard notes:

> As opposed to the participants of the street revival meeting, Sonny, through his non-lamenting meta-narrative of jazz, claims for himself and communicates to others, most notably the narrator, the agency some of the more crystallized forms of the blues deny, an agency without which the Civil Rights Movement could not have happened...Written in 1957, the "blues text" of "Sonny's Blues" exemplifies Baldwin's commitment to being a "trained" critic of the contesting intracultural narratives that have had profound impacts on

the consciousness and destinies of African Americans in twentieth-century urban life.[22]

"Sonny's Blues" is a story of defiance, freedom, improvisation, and hope. Baldwin reminds his readers that the way we "play the music" defines how we "listen to the music." Sonny's music provides him hope because he can improvise and rebel against those conditions that led him into his predicaments of slavery to drugs and life in a racist society. Sonny is a hero, one who stands within and offers a voice of change, of improvisation. Not content to merely lament his lot in life, he finds new music, new ways of expressing hope. His song is one of freedom, of resurrection.

The movement from death to life, from bondage to freedom transforms Sonny and his brother. The transformation cannot happen without the help and hope of others. Sonny cannot experience freedom simply by his own will; the change happens when he lets go into the waters with the guidance and support of Creole and the other musicians. Freedom allows us to break away from those conditions that enslave us. Sonny didn't want to be just any musician; he wanted to be a jazz musician, to play *with* jazz musicians. His dream comes true. Listening to the music of "Sonny's Blues" sets free those who have been captive. When we enter the chaotic waters, we wade in deep and far. But we come through to the other side as an indigo light spreads its rays of hope in our lives.

Exploration of the Idioms and Cultures of the Blues

The blues are rooted in the early traditions, cultures, and music of African Americans. Scholars explain the music's origins in several ways. James Cone traces the roots of the blues to the "slave-seculars" of early generations of African American communities in this country. These songs express the tensions and skepticism experienced by black slaves who "found it difficult to take seriously anything suggesting the religious faith of white preachers."[23] Difficulties arise when black people try to connect their experience of slavery and oppression to themes in white Christian theology. White Christians used these themes to legitimize slavery. The blues express these same difficulties with the culture. However, the blues do not resort to "otherworldly" answers but respond with "this worldly" answers. Cone argues that in spirit the blues and spirituals share the same ancestral history, but express it in different ways. "The blues are 'secular spirituals.' They are *secular* in the sense that they confine their attention solely to the immediate and affirm the bodily expression of black soul, including its sexual manifestations. They are *spirituals* because they are impelled by the search for the truth of black experience."[24] Both the spirituals and the blues help create a fuller understanding of black experience as a search for the truth.

Stephen Asthma uses Cone's work to explain that the blues and gospel music have been closely tied together in several ways: "in chord progressions, pentatonic scales, rhythmic structures, and so forth—but the two genres have been consistently characterized as representative of the sacred and the profane dimensions of African-American culture."[25] This characterization, however, may be oversimplified. The blues are a cultural critique of the mainstream church community, a kind of "Promethean resistance to the acquiescent values...Blues mythology is rich with cultural rebellion."[26] The blues provide a cultural critique of mainstream Christianity and the imperialistic values that denigrate blues music.

Angela Davis, in *Blues Legacies and Black Feminism,* examines the cultural aesthetic that women blues artists have created. Davis notes that they came to prominence during the early twentieth century to "help create a new black consciousness."[27] While the spirituals and gospel music expressed freedom in religious terms, the blues were sung about a more "immediate and accessible freedom."[28] In particular, the blues "registered sexuality as a tangible expression of freedom" and they became characterized as "secular spirituals."[29] The church condemned the blues as "devil's music" because they "drew upon and incorporated sacred consciousness and thereby posed a serious threat to religious attitudes."[30] The blues replaced some religious experiences of community, and women's voices became the missionaries of the new music. Davis notes that women blues singers "were performing as professional artists and attracting large audiences of revival-like gatherings."[31]

Similar displacement of traditional religious communities and new leadership by women are now also occurring in ministry and theological arenas. As women's voices chant the liturgy and preach sermons, some Christians demonize their presence. Unwelcome in many parts of the church, these "other" theological voices often sound strident and dissonant to traditional ears. For those whose investment is in preserving the familiar old music, with the same old tunes, these new voices will not be allowed to sing.

Women have long been identified as the devil's tempters. Davis explains that, as the blues singers threatened others in their communities, the sexuality of women clergy threatens a male-dominated form of traditional Christianity. Davis notes:

> The blues women openly challenged the gender politics implicit in traditional cultural relationships of marriage and heterosexual love relationships. Refusing, in the blues tradition of raw realism, to romanticize romantic relationships, they instead exposed the stereotypes and explored the contradictions of those relationships. By so doing, they redefined women's "place." They forged and memorialized images of tough, resilient, and independent women who were afraid neither of their own vulnerability nor of defending their right to be respected as autonomous human beings.[32]

The legacies of blues women, like those of women priests, is to offer a new voice, a different model of being free in the world. Freedom arises from resiliency, from a passion to be immersed in the raw reality of this world. The heart of the gospel is about being free. Slavery captures people when they become trapped by traditions and cultural images that limit their humanity. The power of the blues is found in its use of sacred themes and secular voices to challenge the real demons of the world—abuse, slavery, dehumanization. These new priests remind us that the church is in a world that "has come of age."

Albert Murray, a literary critic and social commentator, explains that the blues are a highly stylized form of expression. The blues idiom gives one a sense of human grandeur, an artistic expression of universal worth. While the blues are rooted in black experience of suffering and evil, they must be seen as an expression of a stylized form of art. Murray is careful to warn white students of black culture that what makes a "blues idiom musician is not the ability to express raw emotion with primitive directness, as is so often implied, but rather the mastery of elements of aesthetics peculiar to U.S. Negro music."[33] Murray explains that the origin of blues music is not in some "raw experience" but in the experience of being with other artists. We can see this same thought expressed by Baldwin in "Sonny's Blues." Suffering is not exalted for its own sake; singing the old songs doesn't necessarily move one to "new music." But Sonny discovers through his art a new way of expressing his suffering. "In other words, the origin for art is likely to be art itself."[34] Other artists are the community from which the music grows. This stylization in turn shapes the community's members. Thus, at the end of the story, Sonny is shaped by the community's music.

Creativity is rooted in the styles of the musicians. Community is essential to the way the music develops. While the blues tend to be individualized, the music evokes the styles of other musicians. Murray explains:

> They derive most directly from styles of other musicians who play the blues and who were infinitely more interested in evoking or simulating raw emotion than in releasing it—and whose "primitiveness" is to be found not so much in the directness of their expression as in their pronounced emphasis on stylization. In art both agony and ecstasy are matters of stylization.[35]

Other African American musicians are the inspiration for developing the blues idiom and not some "collective reaction to the experience of slavery and segregation as such."[36] Murray tries to dispel the myth that blacks can only create good music if they are oppressed. Black experience is not equivalent to "black misery."[37] He offers instead the analogy of Duke Ellington's transforming the "raw experience of American Negroes into what Malraux calls style."[38] Thus, the music of Ellington rises above experience as such and undergoes a transformation into art.

The blues do not legitimize or romanticize suffering; the blues resist it. This is a communal art, art created by the ensemble. The music is transformed from individual experience into the "artistic tradition of mankind at large."[39] Sonny's blues are not just his individual experiences but help give voice to his experiences within a community. The individual, though the hero of the music, is integrally shaped by the ensemble. Communal support for individual expression is experienced in the playing of the music. Thus, individuals may express their laments, but they do so with other voices.

The processes of creativity and transformation are at the roots of the blues experience. To be human is to improvise. Improvisation enables people to rise above the raw experience of life and transform it into art. This is precisely what happens in "Sonny's Blues." Sonny's idiomatic music tells us who he really is. He becomes a hero, depicted with grace and style. Murray writes,

> *Improvisation is the ultimate human (i.e., heroic) endowment.* It is, indeed; and even as flexibility or the ability to swing (or to perform with grace under pressure) is the key to that unique competence which generates the self-reliance and thus the charisma of the hero, and even as infinite alertness-become-dexterity is the functional source of the magic of all master craftsmen, so may skill in the art of improvisation be that which both will enable contemporary man to be at home with his sometimes tolerable but never quite certain condition of *not* being at home in the world and will also dispose him to regard his obstacles and frustrations as well as his achievements in terms of adventure and romance.[40]

The story of Sonny ends with improvisation as the "ultimate human endowment." He indeed adapts, learns self-reliance, and learns to be at home in a world that does not always want him. Life can be inhospitable; we can be displaced and homeless. Instead of falling victim to those conditions, Sonny adapts to his world with creative dexterity, playing tunes that allow him to really "play the music." Likewise, Sonny's music entices those around him to really listen, to pay attention to their own melody, to catch the drift of the combo. Sonny's blues teach us how to "swing, to perform with grace under pressure." Baldwin's story is about finding adventure in a risky world and falling in love with the music that we are freed to play.

What the Blues Say about the Themes of Suffering and Evil

What do the blues say about the themes of suffering and evil? Many theologians and philosophers offer "answers" to the problem of evil in either logical or existential forms. Many of these so-called answers float like clouds above the pain and suffering that real people are actually experiencing. While conceptual arguments are important in theological and philosophical discussions, the problem of suffering and evil cannot be answered with abstractions. The voices of those who sing the blues offer a correction to the abstraction. Cone explains:

> What is the explanation of black suffering in the blues? It is important to observe that the blues, like the spirituals, were not written or sung for the purpose of answering the "problem of evil." They merely describe the reality of black suffering without seeking to devise philosophical solutions for the problem of absurdity. In this sense, the blues are existential; that is they assume that reality inherent in historical existence and not in abstract essence. That is why there is much emphasis on the concrete restrictions placed on the black community, and why color is a dominant theme of the blues.[41]

Blues describe experience; they are not "answers" as such to the problem of evil. Abstractions can leave those responsible for suffering and evil in the "clouds" because they are unresponsive to and detached from the experiences of those who are suffering. The music of the blues concretizes the answer as a description of reality that calls for resistance, transformation, and change.

The blues critique the culture that supported and legitimized slavery. These "secular spirituals" give voice to the frustrations that black people felt at the hands of whites. The blues tell a story. This music expresses through thinking and feeling the raw data of life in this alien country. "Black music, then, is not an artistic creation for its own sake; rather it tells us about the feeling and thinking of an African people, and the kinds of mental adjustments they had to make in order to survive in an alien land."[42] The music is not an abstraction; that is, an "artistic creation for its own sake." The words and music of the blues evoke feelings, thoughts, and experiences.

While slavery is the historical background for the blues, it is a music to rise above the conditions of slavery. "Slavery is the historical background out of which the blues were created. From a theological perspective, the blues are closely related to the 'slave seculars.'"[43] The blues are a "secular" answer to the problem of suffering and evil. That answer does not exist in some otherworldly escape hatch but in the concrete particulars of this world. As Cone notes, "It is not that the blues reject God; rather they ignore God by embracing the joys and sorrows of life, such as those of a man's relationship with his woman, a woman with her man."[44] One can easily understand the frustration with the otherworldly answers given by white Christians to the problems experienced by blacks. The blues offer a new way, another voice. By ignoring the God of white Christianity, the blues give voice to the details of daily life.

Asthma exposes the flaws within white Christian theology that legitimized and sanctioned slavery. He claims that the blues, as secular music, challenge the sacred themes of Christian voices. The blues challenge the Christian theological presuppositions of human depravity and of original sin. Asthma's description of original sin might be a bit theologically simplistic, but in actual practice his description is accurate for the reality of many Christians. He explains:

> According to the doctrine of original sin—a central component of all Christianity—human beings are born in a state of depravity; we are all marked with some offending metaphysical stain that makes us spiritually impure. In other words, no one is innocent and no one deserves happiness. Human beings are guilty simply because of their being born human.[45]

Thus, the manifestation of original sin is pride, which is the refusal to recognize that one is sinful and unclean, creating an attitude that we must be apologetic for life. This attitude even encourages us to accept our suffering in life because we deserve it. This apologetic stance in life, contends Asthma, led to a reinforcement of suffering for the slave community. In contrast, Asthma offers the model of the blues artist as a rebellious hero who sings her protest and challenges the slave ethic:

> It is with this spirit of protest and resolve that the blues artist challenges the so-called slave ethic of mainstream morality. While the Christian is in need of redemption and forgiveness, the blues artist boasts of personal power and rebels against authority and convention.[46]

Asthma's picture of the blues artist as rebellious hero coincides with the picture of the blues hero drawn by Albert Murray.

Singing the blues is a strategy for rising above the experiences of suffering and evil. "The blues were techniques of survival and expressions of courage."[47] Improvisation in blues leads to skills of being at home in the world when the world may not want us. Sonny's courage is expressed in his attempt to play again, to enter the deep waters. His music is a metaphor for learning how to swing with grace under pressure. The grace comes from the support of the community, from his own fierce passion for the music. Grace comes when he lets go into the waters of the music.

The Blues as a Metaphor for the Cross and Resurrection

How can the blues serve as a metaphor for the cross and resurrection? We return to the question we asked at the beginning. What kind of a difference does the cross and resurrection of Jesus Christ make to the world? "How is it that God in the life and death of Jesus acted to confront evil in a decisive and redemptive manner?"[48] The blues have taught me something about the heart of the Christian faith. *Sonny's blues become the metaphor for re-visioning the central symbol of the Christian tradition.* God in Jesus Christ does not magically rescue us from the evils and sufferings of this world and transport us to some heavenly realm. Instead, we are given the grace by God to learn how to resist, confront, and transform the suffering and evil we encounter in our life. We are given the grace to swing, to perform with grace under pressure.

Ray finds within the tradition a patristic model of the atonement that has often been dismissed by scholars as crude and naive. This model is characterized by the battle between God and Satan, the forces of good and evil. Drawing on the work of Irenaeus and Gregory of Nyssa, she explains that the incarnation is the central theological piece in this theory:

> By becoming incarnate, it was argued, God fooled Satan into thinking that Jesus was just another human being—sinful and subject to death...God "baffled His adversary" the devil and "exhausted the force" of his attack...God has acted not only to reveal the true nature of evil but also to decenter and delegitimate its authority by luring it into exposing its own moral bankruptcy and thus defeating itself, hence opening up the possibility for human beings to escape enslavement to evil.[49]

Ray develops this patristic model by emphasizing that the response by God to evil is to expose it and to empower us to resist evil. She critiques those interpretations of this model that picture God as some kind of cosmic superhero who overcomes evil once and for all. Many atonement theories, including this classic patristic model, portray the act of God's overcoming evil as final. Yet, in this century, the overwhelming evidence is contrary to this. Ray and other feminist theologians rightly note that this once-and-for-all attitude can lead one to a passivity or to a comfortable feeling that everything is already accomplished in victory.[50] In a very similar way, the blues are critical of otherworldly schemes that deny or minimize the suffering and pain of this life.

In both the blues and the voices of feminist theology, I find a similar resolution to this problem, which is to develop a strategy for recognizing evil, naming it, and creatively resisting it. Like Sonny, we must realize that we have to learn how to struggle against evil and not succumb to it. Failure is possible. Liberation from evil comes when we are free to determine that evil no longer determines who we are. Ray explains:

To be liberated from bondage to evil means that evil no longer determines one's being and actions, that one is free to resist evil and to try to reduce it. We are saved not *from* the vicissitudes, vulnerabilities, and inevitable suffering of finite existence, but *for* a particular way of responding to those inevitabilities, a way that, as we will see, Jesus exemplified in his life and death. Redemption, then, is a profoundly this-worldly affair, though it implies a radical transformation of our conception of and place in the world.[51]

Sonny finds his place in the world by responding with grace to the pressures that surround his life. He does so with the support of the ensemble. Sonny's salvation is a movement through the depths of the water, from the chaos to order. Learning to improvise makes Sonny a hero. He is freed from responding to evil as a victim, and freed to help others around him resist evil and suffering. Ray notes that those who live at the margins take what is at hand and make "creative use of what is available to them."[52]

Sonny's music subverts the way things were to bring about the way things might be. He transforms reality through the improvisation of the music. Ray's last comments on liberation from evil are remarkably similar to those of Murray's about improvisation: "To be liberated from evil in a world that remains so clearly in its grasp means refusing to let evil define our options and existence. It means struggling against evil with passion, creativity, cunning, and tenacity, but without violence, without cruelty or hatred, without callous indifference."[53] God endows us with the graceful opportunity to creatively improvise, that is, perform with grace under pressure. Evil is overcome through creative adaptation, by cunning devices. God's message in Jesus Christ is that evil is not the last word. The resurrection is God's creative improvisation, a cunning device to trick the powers of evil.

From Lent to Easter

I return to the season of Lent. For Christians, the cross is always linked to the resurrection. Suffering and death are not the last words. Lent does not leave us at Good Friday. Some Christians would prefer to stay in the shadow of the cross without ever looking toward the resurrection. But we are called not only to die, but to live. If we die with the Lord, we will live with the Lord. Living with God in faith is like listening to Sonny's music. We learn to swing, to perform with grace under pressure. Shaped by the community of faith and by the grace of God, we learn not only to live, but to live well. We step into the waters of our baptism. In the indigo watery depths, we are called daily to die and to rise. We find our chaos transformed into order.

I am beginning another season of Lent, a period of struggle between good and evil, winter and spring, death and life. Lent is teaching me how to live amidst transition, to face ambiguity, to come up against my limits. We mark those limiting experiences of the human condition with a service of the imposition of ashes. The dirty smudge of ashes marks our foreheads with the sign of the cross. We are on a journey to Good Friday. We mark the season of Lent with sacrifice, fasting, and prayerful preparation. Yet, Lent would mean nothing but a celebration of death and misery without the dawning light of the resurrection morning. Lent is a season of paying attention to our creatureliness, of listening to the laments of those in pain, of walking the way of the cross. Lent is a season of transition. From beginnings of ashes we turn and face eastward to the passion, death, and resurrection of Jesus Christ. What kind of music marks the season of Lent to Easter? Of death to resurrection?

I have always been intrigued with Mark's gospel narrative of the crucifixion. Jesus dies with a question on his lips, "My God, my God, why have you forsaken me?" This question from Jesus' mouth echoes the laments of generations. His question is part of the tradition of the lament psalms, of generations of voices whose songs of protest against God and life resonate with the particularities of life's problems and possibilities. Jesus gives voice in painful song to the questions that we are most afraid to ask. Why does God seem so far away when we are most alone? Where are those who love us when we need them?

The lament psalms are the root of songs that Jews and Christians have used for centuries to express their condition in the world. Several years ago I began to listen to the voices of those who sing the blues. Like the lament psalms, the blues protest the problems of pain, suffering, and daily life. "The origin and definition of the blues cannot be understood independent of the suffering that black people endured in the context of white racism."[54] The roots of the blues are not abstractions; they live in the context of a racism that sought to punish and destroy those who were different. From the racism of slavery to the camps of Auschwitz, the theme of the blues won't let us forget where the suffering came from. To forget the source is to miss the music. The blues are an idiom and mode of expression that are an "artistic response to the chaos of life."[55] These secular spirituals create the musical liturgy for the ambiguity of life's in-between times. To listen to the blues is to listen to a metaphor for expressing the Lenten seasons of our lives.

Years ago, when I was first at the seminary, I attended a memorial service for a young man who had committed suicide. This chapel service included a song based on Romans 8 that said that "nothing can separate us from the love of God." This song, sung in a blues/gospel style, reminded me that musicians can be the priests of our lives. Music calls forth the experience of God in ways that the words of sermons cannot. "The 'new priests' of the black community were the blues men and women; and their songs were the blues."[56]

The blues are the song of the whole creation. Surely no scripture passage can better summarize the cosmic cry of creation than the longing of the whole creation in Paul's letter to the Romans. Like a woman groaning in travail, the creation longs to be redeemed from its suffering. As Christians, we must listen to those "secular spirituals," which remind us that abstractions are dangerous. People are concrete, living, breathing experiences. The blues become a strategy for living in the world, not some abstract answer to the problem of evil.

The blues lead to transformation. Something new happens when one engages in the music. The victim is transformed into a hero. Albert Murray explains the relationship between the epic heroes in American literature and the hero in the blues. He compares the contemporary detective story hero to the blues idiom hero: "a nada-confrontation hero, which is also to say, a slapstick hero, not only because of the nature of his quest and certain characteristics of his sensibility, but also because his behavior is so compatible with his circumstances, which are nothing if not slapdash jam-session situation or predicament in the first place."[57] The hero is adaptive to life's crazy terms, improvising on the spot, trusting the ensemble, listening to the music. For Murray, improvisation is what creates a hero. New life requires grace. This could hardly be said better theologically. What God does in the resurrection is to offer us the ability to swing, to perform with grace under pressure.

FEMINIST and liberation theologians offer a clue for listening to different kinds of music when they encourage us to listen to those whose experience begins in Lent, in suffering and pain. In the music of the blues, I hear voices that know the depths of suffering and evil but that confront that evil with resistance and grace.

5

THE LIFE OF THE CHURCH

I have a fine sounding radio mounted on the headboard of my bed. It is tuned to one station, 89.1 on the FM dial. The station is owned by Mt. Hood College and their theme is "The Wide Spectrum of Jazz." The station is unique because it is one of the only stations in the country devoted to jazz…At this very moment I'm listening to "Willow Weep for Me." When I had my first little shop, I moved in a good high fidelity stereo set and I would stack it with music I liked. Customers would come in and often comment on the beautiful music, "That's great music," and I would say, "Oh! You like jazz," and the customer would say, "No! I don't like jazz but I like that." My point is that perhaps the word jazz is not accepted by some people, just as some people won't accept the Bible.

VERN HOLMQUIST[1]

THE DOCTRINE of creation is the beginning point for the story of God's creative and redeeming work in the world. The church's mission is to improvise on that theme anew in each generation.

Worship

Worship is central to the expression of the Christian faith. The liturgy and worship life of communities reflect the very essence of what it means to be called Christian. Therefore, no task is more important than reflection on the nature and purpose of Christian worship. No matter what denomination we come from, the act of worship expresses our connection to God and to one another. Worship reminds us that God, not ourselves, is at the center of our faith. Expressed in traditions passed down through centuries, worship generates community. In communities of faith, the worship life reveals how Christian belief is embodied and lived out daily. One can tell what is important to a congregation by how it worships. It is understandable that many divisions within congregations revolve around issues and styles of worship. For many people, worship is their formal theological education. We know what we believe by how we worship. We must ask ourselves whether the worship in which we engage reflects adequately both the gospel message of the Christian tradition and its applicability to daily life. Word without world is meaningless; world without Word is idolatrous.

Coming from a Lutheran background, I have always understood that the celebration of the sacraments and the preaching of the Word define church. The sacraments and the proclamation of the Word are where the finite meets the infinite, where God meets the world. Music and the visual arts express in symbols this embodied meaning of Word and sacrament. Susan Ross, a Roman Catholic theologian, shares similar sentiments:

> My interest in the arts, particularly music, originally led me to work in sacramental theology. The sacraments are, in a way, 'works of art' for the church—works that are at the same time ordinary and extraordinary, celebrating the transcendent within the immanent. Like music, the sacraments say in gesture, sound, rhythm, and word, that which cannot be said otherwise. I have always felt a deep connection with these ancient rituals…But this deep connection has always included a sour note. My femaleness means that I am, to some extent, an interloper in these rituals. Of all the sacraments, only one requires the presence of a woman.[2]

For many like Ross and me, worship is an ambivalent and ambiguous experience and expression. The music of faith runs deep in our bodies, often conveying deep and strong sentiments. Singing a rousing verse of "A Mighty Fortress Is Our God" is the way I learned in my gut what it meant to be Lutheran. Yet I also learned that hymn in a congregation whose leadership did not believe that women should be ordained or have leadership roles in the congregation. The inconsistencies are more than a "sour note." The whole composition sounds off-key. What do we do about the fundamental harmony of the faith when it excludes and dominates other voices?

The very center of the church expressed in Word and sacrament is also the center that marginalizes those considered "other" and leaves the rest of the created order as mere backdrop to the "more important" work of human salvation. We need to refocus the center of our faith and draw boundaries that will include instead of exclude. The real worship issues are not really contemporary versus traditional. We have discovered that those boundaries can be very divisive. The issues lie in the nature of the composition and the character of the ensemble. As Robert McAfee Brown reminds us, we need a theology in a new key. My claim is that perhaps we need not only a new theology, but also a new worship in a new paradigm. How do we begin? Perhaps we can learn again from listening to those whose traditions begin at the margins and whose ensembles by nature of the music include all as participants. Like musicians playing the notes of a classic tune with the grace of improvisers, Christians need to find ways to maintain the balance of tradition with the present culture. The model of improvisation offers one strategy for accomplishing this goal for Christian worship of listening in a new key, of creating new ways for being the community of God in worship. Jazz and the blues offer Christianity a new metaphor for "playing the music."

What is the relationship between a liturgy and a theology based on improvisation? Because worship is central to Christian identity, we must explore how worship can be interpreted using the metaphor of creativity and improvisation. How do we compose our worship? Are we more like a jazz ensemble, a slick prepackaged program, or a passive audience in a concert? The connections and questions are important for several reasons. First, the creation has been eclipsed as part of the "ensemble" in most liturgical settings. Although references to the created order and God as creator exist, they are not central. We may have our obligatory Earth Day or Ecology worship service, or even sing rousing verses of "Earth and All Stars." But that is not enough. If we ignore creation, we diminish the wide arena of God's creative and redeeming grace. Second, worship for many congregations is still a passive experience. The pastors do most of the "work." Congregational members just play their parts and follow the maestro. How can we create more participatory and less hierarchical ways of worshiping? Third, worship often sanctions the cultural status quo. We become complacent with repeating the same prayers and expecting the same comfortable arrangement with God. Annie Dillard remarks, "Many times in Christian churches I have heard the pastor say to God, 'All your actions show your wisdom and love.' Each time, I reach in vain for the courage to rise and shout, 'That's a lie!'—just to put things on a solid footing."[3] What we have learned about improvisation might enable us to have the courage to join with Dillard in protest at those places where the incongruity is too great. A theological model of improvisation *might* free us from the constraints of some of the battles we currently face in our worship and liturgical traditions.

What Is Our Situation?

Our current worship climate reflects the problem of how to integrate the elements of Christian tradition within the experience and culture of contemporary life. What kind of relationship should the church have with contemporary culture? In much of the practice of American religion, Christian worship is wrapped in all the trappings of a consumeristic, fast-paced, individualistic culture. Church leaders are prodded to increase membership, to increase monies given, to buy newer and better buildings, to adapt to all the new technologies. Although some of the new church growth language is surely promising, much of it can detract from the very critique that the church needs to offer to the culture in which it is so tightly enmeshed. How does worship both express cultural forms and yet also offer a prophetic critique of those cultural expressions that detract from the message of the gospel? What are the current worship wars between contemporary and traditional services all about? What is the purpose of worship? Who should lead, plan, and attend worship? These questions are rooted in Christianity's struggles about the heart and purpose of worship.

From Dachau to Disney

This last year was one of extremes. My professional meeting of the American Academy of Religion was in Walt Disney World in Orlando, Florida. For six days in November, I spent most of my time walking between two hotels and seeing the reflections of Disney World in the distance. The meals were extraordinarily ordinary and outrageously expensive. The hotels were gauche; the halls were lined with beachlike patterns with a sandlike carpet. Many of us concluded that theology already has a certain "Mickey-Mouse" flavor without adding to it. Although Disney has entertained generations of children (me included), I couldn't help but wonder about such a setting for a national meeting of theologians and religious studies teachers. Maybe it was more appropriate than I realized. Perhaps our theological commitments are no different from the marketing ploys Disney uses to entertain. I can't help but think of Martin Luther's criticism of the relationship between the mass and the market. Is there need for reformation?

Later that summer, at Lutheran retreat center Holden Village, high in the Cascade Mountains, I taught two weeks of theology to clergy and laity. We had great discussions, and I learned a great deal. During one session, we were thinking about the nature of worship and our contemporary culture. How could we be critical of our market-driven culture and yet also realize that we need to appeal to people's cultural sensibilities in order to reach them in worship settings? This discussion was not an easy one. Some wanted to try new ways to market the worship service so that we could attract those who are not currently attending or those who find church "boring" (as the child of a friend of mine says about church). Others felt that simply to cave in to people's consumeristic tastes gives away the gospel's critical edge toward the culture.

One of the clergy in attendance brought to our attention a brochure that was announcing a new conference in Disney World on worship. Those who would attend were promised "sound Biblical principles" with "proven Disney techniques" for attracting people to church. Much like Luther in the time in which he lived, we face the danger of selling our souls to the seduction of bigger and better. As the pastor read from the brochure, gasps were audible in the room. This clergyperson noted that such marketing was tantamount to blasphemy. I agreed. Doesn't Jesus turn over the tables in the temple? Later that evening, another clergyperson stopped me and challenged my viewpoint. She had attended such conferences and had found them very helpful. She said the church needed to find ways to reach people, and this was one opportunity to find such ways. Was I too traditional for such new ideas? I had never thought of myself as conservative in such a discussion about worship. Was I just another middle-aged, middle-class theologian defending the status quo? I wondered.

Then I thought about another image that has stayed with me all summer. I spent sixteen days as chaperone with two hundred high school students on a musical tour of Europe. During one of our free days, we spent the morning in Dachau. Hardly Disney World. I was worried about what it would be like to go through Dachau: Could I visit such a horrific place, especially with two hundred loud high school students? After we left the buses, we walked into the entrance and directly into a theater, where we watched a video on the history of Dachau. Within a minute or two, the crowd of students and chaperones was speechless. We left in silence and watched while another large group of loud students entered the theater. They would leave changed too.

What followed was more than I had imagined or expected. I have read Elie Wiesel, talked to friends whose families were exterminated in the camps, watched films about the Holocaust. Nothing could have prepared me for the horror I felt that day, not like a summer flick but more like an insidious sickness that creeps slowly into the skin and doesn't leave. The horror is still there. What stuck with me was not only the horror of the mass exterminations but also the petty terrors of daily life. The Nazis had an extreme obsession with keeping the camps clean. Prisoners were often tortured in the public square for leaving dust in their room or not making their beds exactly right. To make things even crazier, the SS guards would often enter a barracks right before inspection and tear things apart, making it impossible for the prisoners to make things right. I thought again about my Lutheran background and how Luther's writings had been used by the Nazis to justify persecution of the Jews. A different kind of blasphemy.

What do I do with Disney and Dachau? They were parts of the same summer, the same experience of what Christians can do in a modern world with their culture. Both seem blasphemous, but for very different reasons. Dachau is a blasphemous reminder that the church can never forget its complicity in such horrors. My own Lutheran tradition is complicit in helping to justify the extermination of millions of Jews. How do I live in a culture and live as a Christian? What is the relationship between Christianity and culture? Other theologians such as the Niebuhrs have helped us to reflect on these issues. But again I thought of these two images of Disney and Dachau, and I thought of worship. What did all of this have to do with one another? What is the situation for North American Christians, particularly those of us who have been in privileged, homogeneous traditions? I can only speak from that perspective and hope to learn from others. How can we live as a church and a community faithful to the gospel and also be a witness to the world? The answer seems to reside in careful reflection on both the message of the gospel and the nature of the world.

Worship Wars

In many American churches, people divide and conquer over worship styles and liturgical rituals. We debate whether to stand or sit during communion, whether to use incense for festival services, whether we should reword the prayers and creeds, and whether to learn new music or stick with the old favorites. Sunday morning worship becomes the battleground for our personal preferences. What I have discovered is that much of the battle boils down to how "it used to be" or how "I want it to be." I'm as guilty as anyone of wanting a worship experience that fits my needs and interests. However, I can't help but wonder if the way we worship indicates how we understand the purpose and goal of the Christian faith. Is Christianity merely a religion of personal preferences that offers *me* comfort and salvation? Or is the vision broader? How do we look for new voices, new ways of being in the world without collapsing Christianity completely into the cultures that surround us? How do we worship in a postmodern world? How do we avoid Disney and Dachau? We need different ways to mend the divisions.

For several years I have had the experience of worshiping in two different congregations: Roman Catholic and Lutheran. At my own Lutheran congregation, worship styles have divided the congregation for years. In fact, the congregation has even been on the front page of the local newspaper. With a baptized membership of five thousand, the congregation offers traditional or contemporary worship. What I have noticed is that the congregation is really two—marked by which service you attend. Unfortunately, those barriers are often marked by age, and possibly even by class. In either case, the services have often turned into battlegrounds or turf wars about the church's identity and mission. We haven't been able to resolve the impasse. I'm convinced that part of the problem is that we don't understand the congregation's mission and identity. Consequently, we don't really understand the point of worship, which is to "go and serve the Lord."

In contrast, the situation is handled differently at the Roman Catholic congregation. On any given Sunday, members do not know what kind of music will be part of the service. Musical groups are rotated with the hope that people will attend the service for its own sake and not merely for a particular musical performance. Sometimes a cantor sings. Other times there is a small group or an organist. Consequently, the congregation is not as divided along stylistic concerns, and one can always count on experiencing the form of the mass. The congregation has let the form of the mass free them to explore and worship in new ways that do not always divide the congregation.

Both churches have different problems and attempt to solve them through their own traditional resources. Roman Catholic worship has changed radically since Vatican II, and in many circles their liturgical reform has shaped the scope of ecumenical worship. Lutherans struggle to fit with tradition and faithfulness the Lutheran notion that the church is always reforming (*ecclesia semper reformanda*). How do we maintain continuity with the past and yet remain vital and alive in the twenty-first century? Marva Dawn, a Lutheran theologian, asks the same question: "We must ask if church effectiveness and preserved traditions are mutually exclusive and whether traditions prevent creativity. What is lost in the process if we throw away traditions for the sake of success and novelty?"[4] Creativity, as we have noted, is not simply novelty for its own sake. Creativity apart from tradition is rootless; tradition apart from creativity is dead. They must be viewed in a reciprocal relationship where they mutually enhance each other.

We in the church have not often handled this tension very well. "Contemporary worship" is seen as a break with the constraints of the past; traditional worship finds the roots of tradition freeing. Perhaps they need to listen to each other. Dawn remarks,

> Even in the church—and especially in the "worship wars"— we see what Lasch calls "the fashionable sneer that now automatically greets every loving recollection of the past" and that exploits "the prejudices of a pseudo-progressive society." Historically, however we know that many radical movements drew "strength and sustenance from the myth or memory" of the past.[5]

Many of the great reform movements, from the monastics to the Anabaptists, did not simply abort the past but used it as a source of strength to challenge the current hierarchies and heresies. However, in a culture so dominated by the myth of youth and the seduction of consumerism, we often turn up our nose at anything that is traditional.

How we worship tells a lot about what we think of the importance of worship. In one of her caustic remarks, Dillard offers her critique of worship practices:

> Since "we" have been doing this for 2,000 years, why can we not do it as well as a high school drama club cast can do after

six weeks of rehearsing a play? Not that worship is anything but rehearsable performance and not that a high school play is worship—though drama and liturgy do have some common ancient roots. But people who attend services of prayer and praise, song and action, preaching and the sacraments, often have to endure mumbling and stumbling offputting sorts. This is not how God is to be praised, and this is not what worshipers will put up with for indefinite periods to come.[6]

Dillard's comments are appropriate when we think that worship is not important. Many Christians' only theological training comes through the readings, hymns, prayers, and sermons on Sunday mornings. We cannot afford to ignore the importance of the formative nature of those traditions and their contemporary expressions. On the one hand, worship can appear to be a performance. We simply engage in ecclesiastical or liturgical correctness. Did the pastor bow at the right time; did the congregation stand on the correct verse? On the other hand, if no thought is put into the direction, purpose, and planning of worship, it can turn into bland entertainment with no substance.

So how do we understand the culture in which we worship? The relationship between who we are as church and the context in which we live our daily lives must be explored. Samuel Torvend, a Lutheran liturgical author, explains the culture in which we live and how that relates to worship. His analysis is helpful because it broadens the traditionally narrow focus the church has had on culture and context. The broad context for worship tells us that we are in a cosmic culture, that creation in its broadest sense is our culture. Our place in the world is radically relativized when we realize what a brief time we have been on this earth and how vast the universe is. This view corresponds with our earlier concern that our anthropocentric view has blinded us to the rest of creation. We must expand the ensemble to include all of creation.

Christians must also realize that they worship in a world that is *not,* and has never been, predominantly Christian. This is more obvious in some places in the United States than in others. In Chicago, I lived in a neighborhood with several different seminaries, a variety of religious traditions, and diverse ethnic backgrounds. I was very aware that I was not in the majority. I thought about my faith differently in that context. Now, in South Dakota people just assume that everyone is Christian. That has caused me to rethink what it means to be Christian in a world where one's assumptions may harm or discriminate against those who are not like the majority. Torvend remarks: "In some communities today, the overwhelming majority of people who ever lived on the earth have never had any contact with the Christian church."[7] To ignore the religious and cultural diversity of our world is to ignore and impoverish the context in which we live out our lives as Christians.

In the Euro-American world where Western Christianity has dominated, we face a time when Christianity is fading as the dominant institution (if it ever really was). People now have "the recognition that Western Christianity dwells in a post-Christian culture where the church and its leaders are no longer regarded as primary authorities in what were largely homogeneous communities."[8] So how does the church understand itself in such a world? Some retreat to the "past" of homogeneity to find protection from the new world. Others celebrate the loss of a center and claim that nothing matters anymore. Others try to find uniqueness without celebrating imperialism. Torvend opts for the middle way:

> It is a view that rejects the grammar of exclusion without denying the uniqueness of a truly open yet critical Christian witness in the world. In this view, the *church is a unique sign established by God among the people of the earth to show what God has done and is continuing to do, whether openly or hiddenly, for all human beings.*[9]

The church can be a sign that walks a different way through the rocky terrain of absolutism and relativism. But now the tough questions remain, What has God done and what does God continue to do? Can the liturgy help us to answer this?

Culturally, we are tied to the marketplace. This hasn't necessarily changed in some ways since Luther's time of the Reformation, when he criticized the Roman Catholic hierarchy for succumbing to the commercialism of the times. The Reformation supposedly began over the controversy of indulgences. The papacy was preying on people's fears about their eternal destiny. For a small pittance, German peasants could shorten their departed relatives' years in purgatory. Meanwhile, on the backs of German peasants, the clerical hierarchy was financing the construction of St. Peter's Basilica in Rome. Luther remarks on the relationship between worship and the marketplace:

> The faith of this sacrament has become utterly extinct, and the holy sacrament has been turned into mere merchandise, a market, and a profit-making business. Hence participations, brotherhoods, intercessions, merits, anniversaries, memorial days and the like wares are bought and sold, traded and bartered, in the church.[10]

Luther was not against "external additions" in their proper place. But when they were used to turn people from the true message of the gospel in Christ Jesus as a free gift, they had become an unnecessary expense on people's consciences.

Torvend harkens to this same criticism of our culture: "When one reads the Gospel narratives, however, it becomes clear that entertaining the masses or soothing the religious establishment found no room in the pattern of Jesus' life."[11] And from Dawn: "The contemporary demand to find a 'marketing niche' actually threatens genuine Christian community, for the purpose of true worship is to offer God what will be pleasing to God."[12] We can turn the gospel into a commodity that can be bought or sold. Although we may not resort to selling indulgences to free our relatives from purgatory, we have other ways of packaging the gospel so that it can be bought and sold on the ecclesiastical marketplace. The "marketing niche" reinforces an individualistic notion of church that is tied critically to the consumeristic notion of buying to satisfy one's desires. The gospel of Jesus Christ challenges the notion that we can buy our way into some sort of relationship with God. The tables in our temples should be overturned.

We try to adapt our liturgy and music to the feel-good, youthful exuberance of today's culture. But life is much more ambiguous, dangerous, and problematic than our liturgies often let us express. Joseph Sittler explains the adaptation of traditional music to the happy mood of our overly optimistic and simplistic culture. He says,

Traditional musical settings had a variety of forms, but they were all characterized by gravity. I'm not sure you can be grave with the time beat this generation likes. I remember an old Sam Johnson statement that the jollity of the clergy much displeased him. Well, much contemporary liturgy is just too jolly! In the Christian faith there is certainly a mood of celebration and thanksgiving. But when one gets beyond the age of 25 or so, the celebrative mood is no longer adequate to one's deepening awareness of life's ambiguities. The God of our worship is indeed Lord of the Dance; but there are nondanceable requirements that he is obliged to satisfy. So this jollification of the liturgy is an appropriate mode for some occasions; it is bitterly inappropriate for others…There is something in the old chants of the church that brought a necessary audible balance to the self-incurvature of contemporary Christianity, and I very much lament its loss.[13]

Liturgy must reflect the complexity of life: joy and sorrow, life and death, anger and happiness, pain and pleasure. Worship brings our experiences to God so that God can bring comfort to the grieving, joy to the sorrowful, healing to those in pain. We impoverish ourselves and our faith if we eliminate the complexities and seek only to simplify, to "jollify."

Christians need to find a way to maintain the balance of tradition with current culture. Dawn comments, "Again we see the critical need for a very careful dialectical balance—keeping the heritage of the faith and offering it in new forms faithful to that heritage."[14] Of course, the difficult question that we must eventually face in this discussion is, What exactly is the heritage of the faith that must find new forms and yet remain faithful? This question has been part of the very heritage that is ours to inherit. Questions about experimentation are questions about the relevance of the tradition. These are also questions raised in the arts, particularly jazz.

Albert Murray—A Reflection on the Jazz Idiom

The issues of tradition are prevalent in any discipline or art that struggles with adaptation and experimentation. Albert Murray notes, "Essentially, questions about experimentation in the arts are also questions about the relevance of tradition. They are questions, that is to say, about the practical application of traditional elements to contemporary problem situations. Hence they are also questions about change and continuity."[15] These same issues surface in jazz traditions as well. The arts try to find ways to link to the tradition within their own contemporary cultures. Often, the success of the music is the critical balance walked between change and continuity, tradition and novelty. The jazz idiom, as in other artistic forms, exemplifies many of the same questions the church faces as it seeks to worship.

Albert Murray's poetic imagination links fiction and music to challenge the way we understand the purpose of the arts. Using all kinds of artists, from Duke Ellington to Ernest Hemingway, Thomas Mann to Andre Malraux, Murray defines the creative process as the social process by which transformation of the present leads into the hope of the future. The creative process builds on the great works of past epochs and can never entirely ignore or lose the past from which it came. The arts must struggle with the nature of humanity, the complexity of experience, and the ethical demands in life. Murray states that the fundamental problem involved in every literary composition (and he would include all the arts, especially music) is "the functional relevance of literary tradition to the immediate requirements of vernacular communication."[16] The problem faced by all art is how to incorporate the past into the living present. Tradition is part of the artist's environment. In fact, it is tradition that brings the present most fully alive for the artist.

Murray's analysis of the creative process centers on the relationship between experimentation and the relevance of tradition. That which endures lives because it works; it brings the past into the living moment of the present. Survival is the specific focus of tradition and experimentation. What will continue? What will change? Murray challenges the notion that experimentation is antitraditional; in fact, he notes that "it actually serves the best interests of tradition, which after all, is that which continues in the first place."[17] Murray's definition of experimentation is improvisation:

> Perhaps a better word for experimentation as it actually functions in the arts is improvisation. In any case, it is for the writer, as for the musician in a jam session, that informal trial

and error process by means of which the tradition adapts itself to change, or renews itself through change. It is, that is to say, the means by which the true and tested in the tradition regenerates itself in the vernacular.[18]

Tradition is alive as it becomes embodied in the life, culture, words, and experience of the present moment. Tradition becomes alive as it works in the present lives of those who adapt. The reason tradition can remain alive is that it renews itself through the experience of those whose words and deeds are interpreting it.

What is the purpose of experimentation? Is improvisation attempted merely for its own sake? Murray notes that improvisation is not an escape from or a rejection of the past, but a "confrontation with the present" and the "projecting [of] an image of man (and of human possibility) that is *intrinsically* revolutionary. Such an image is likely to be automatically at radical odds with the status quo."[19] Improvisation is a social process that challenges the complacency of the present moment by its appropriation of the past as static, dead, antiquated. Improvisation builds on the past to challenge the complacency of the present and revolutionize the future. Tradition dies when it sanctifies the status quo. Improvisation enlivens when it is at radical odds with the status quo. That which is experimental must be adequate to the complexities of human experience in its time and place. Improvisation is transformation.

A Historical Case Study—Improvisation and Reformation

No one was more aware of the problems that liturgical reform could cause than Luther. He struggled not only theologically but also pastorally with the innovations that came with the Reformation. The Reformation was fundamentally a question of authority. For Luther, the study of scripture and the worship of God should be rooted in the people of God and not in the hands of the clergy. Worship was false and the papacy tyrannical when it led people away from God in Jesus Christ, substituting human authority for divine authority. "The very highest worship of God is that we ascribe to him truthfulness, righteousness, and whatever else should be ascribed to one who is trusted."[20]

Luther's most famous writings against the papacy laid the ax to many of the ideas conceived and practiced within the first thousand years of institutional Christianity. In three of his most famous treatises, Luther wrote in protest against the abuses of the laity by the papacy. What is revolutionary about these treatises is Luther's use of the tradition itself to create revolutionary understandings of and practices in the church. In his essay "To the Christian Nobility of the German Nation," Luther attacks three walls constructed by the Romanists: (1) Spiritual power is above temporal power; (2) only the Pope can interpret scripture; and (3) only the Pope can summon a council.[21]

To challenge this first wall, Luther draws on the priesthood of all believers to claim that all Christians are spiritual. "All Christians are truly of the spiritual estate, and there is no difference among them except that of office."[22] Since we are all baptized into the priesthood of believers, priests are nothing other than officeholders. We all share in the work of Christ through our various vocations. Luther's development of the doctrine of baptism roots his argument in the reformation of the hierarchy of the papacy. Temporal authority can exercise its authority over all; whoever is guilty, is guilty.

Luther destroys the second wall with similar scriptural and theological arguments. He notices that while the Romanists want to be masters of the scriptures, many of them have never really studied scripture. For Luther, the issue of the hierarchical Roman power is challenged by the spirit of freedom found in the gospel. The gospel frees us from the abuses of institutional power. He also cites the creed with which we claim that "I believe in the holy Christian church." No single individual has the right to interpret scripture on behalf of the entire church. Since all are priests in Christ, all people have the right and gift to study scripture and test matters of faith.

The third wall is torn down by Luther's notion that there is no basis in scripture that the pope alone can call a council. All Christians are called to be involved in matters of the faith. Luther's critique of the papacy is centered once again on the authority of the church. He reverses the top-down hierarchy of the papacy and offers a bottom-up metaphor of the power of the laity freed in Christ Jesus. Luther notes, "There is no authority in the church except to promote the good."[23] No Christian authority can do anything against Christ. Therefore, the pope cannot call a council alone. The power of the church belongs in the common people, in the laity. Luther's image of the priesthood of all believers, rooted in the tradition of baptism, revolutionizes the hierarchical power of the Romanists.

In his essay "The Babylonian Captivity of the Church," Luther challenges the theological and practical views of the sacraments— the heart of the medieval church. Luther uses the biblical image of the Babylonian captivity of the Jews to show how Christians in medieval Europe were tyrannized and carried away by the papacy. Luther challenges three captivities of the Roman church: (1) withholding of the cup from the laity, (2) the doctrine of transubstantiation, and (3) the sacrifice of the mass. While Luther acknowledges the human authority of the papacy in sacramental practices, he challenges and denies papal authority's being divine. The church substitutes itself for God. Regarding these sacramental abuses, Luther remarks that "it was not the church which ordained these things, but the tyrants of the churches, without the consent of the church, which is the people of God."[24] The sacraments belong to the church: to the laity, the priesthood of all believers.

In other writings, Luther introduced the vernacular into the mass, challenging the intellectual elitism of the Latin mass. One of the most famous contributions of the Reformation was his translation of scripture into German, the language of the common people. For this contribution, Luther has been listed as one of the most important people of the millennium. Luther explains:

> The Holy Spirit did not act like that in the beginning. He did not wait till all the world came to Jerusalem and studied Hebrew, but gave manifold tongues for the office of the ministry, so that the apostles could preach wherever they might go. I prefer to follow this example. It is also reasonable that the young should be trained in many languages; for who knows how God may use them in times to come? For this purpose our schools were founded.[25]

The Holy Spirit is what enlivens the Christian tradition. Like Luther, Albert Murray expresses the role of improvisation as the regeneration of the tradition: "It is, that is to say, the means by which the true and tested in the traditional regenerates itself in the vernacular." The power of tradition is its revolutionary shape in the language of the common people. Murray's insight about the vernacular can be applicable for many of the arts, including liturgical expressions. Luther's use of the vernacular for liturgy and scripture was not to jettison tradition but to reform it through the changes proposed. In this way, Luther could claim that the very best of tradition was still being preserved.

Was Luther revolutionary enough? Did his image of the priesthood of all believers go far enough? Too far? For some involved in the Reformation, he was too conservative, not throwing enough of the baby out with the bathwater. Yet Luther worried about what would happen to people's consciences. Luther explains:

> Nor did I make any innovations. For I have been hesitant and fearful, partly because of the weak in faith, who cannot suddenly exchange an old and accustomed order of worship for a new and unusual one, and more so because of the fickle and fastidious spirits who rush in like unclean swine without faith or reason, and who delight in novelty and tire of it as quickly, when it has worn off. Such people are a nuisance even in other affairs, but in spiritual matters, they are absolutely unbearable.[26]

Timing must be considered, and so must the nature and makeup of the individual congregation. What makes worship work for one setting might not necessarily work for another setting. Luther is right to consider the pastoral concerns. For Luther, change was never merely for its own sake, but always for preserving the freedom of the gospel in Jesus Christ.

A Model for Worship—Improvisation

What Albert Murray and Martin Luther both emphasize is that improvisation has to do with the means by which the true and tested in the traditional regenerates itself in the vernacular. A model of improvisational worship must emphasize those elements that make the traditional come alive: (1) regenerating tradition into the vernacular, (2) confronting the tyrannies of the status quo, and (3) proposing images that are intrinsically revolutionary. The writings of Luther and Murray demonstrate that improvisation by its very nature challenges the way things have been, but more important, they challenge the way things are. The present is transformed by improvisation on the past.

Many of the great Lutheran liturgical organists and composers are also masters of improvisation. I can look forward to a Sunday worship experience or a hymnfest with the same delight I experience at a jazz concert. Recently on a Saturday evening, we went to the new Sioux Falls Washington Pavilion of Arts and Sciences and were transported by the intimacy of Diana Krall and her jazz ensemble. We couldn't believe that for ninety minutes we had been drawn into the music of these four players as if we were in their home. The hall was filled with about thirteen hundred people, but we felt as though they were playing just for us. The solos slipped back and forth with such ease; the ensemble felt one another's every move and nuance. Sometimes church is like that.

Mark Sedio, a superb Lutheran organist and composer, leads worship as Diana Krall plays jazz. The congregation becomes part of the ensemble, and each part of the liturgy becomes an intimate call and response. The organ provides the ground, the transition, the movement through worship. One doesn't need the pastor to stand and interrupt rather loudly, "Please stand and we'll sing Hymn 454; it's printed in your bulletin." Instead, the organ signals the beginning of the hymn, and the congregation knows when to begin. Through verses to the next part of the liturgy, we have a sense that we are part of the experience, part of the music. We write the composition as we sing our parts. From beginning to end, the liturgy unfolds like the improvisational solos in jazz. We sense our parts; we know where we're going. Something deep inside us feels the rhythm of God's music.

Different traditions understand the role of improvisation and creativity in different ways. What may appear as structured and formal may actually lead to creative worship, and what may appear as free and casual may repeat the same experiences week after week. James White examines the theme of creativity within the Free Church tradition and offers a helpful historical perspective on the theme of improvisation and creativity within the liturgy. He locates the Free Church within three historical periods from the Reformation (Continental Anabaptist), through English Puritanism, and to the American Frontier. The latter period is the one on which he concentrates.[27] In contrast to the Anglo-Catholic traditions (which would include Lutheranism, for White), the Free Church is marked by three characteristics: (1) The eucharist is an occasional service (excluding Church of Christ and Disciples of Christ); (2) most of the churches are "antipaedobaptist," that is, the sacraments are viewed as "pious memory exercises" instead of "means of grace"; (3) most churches have a congregational polity.[28] He notes that since nothing is obligatory in liturgical life, and since most do not use service books, such as my own Lutheran tradition, the Free Church tradition has been difficult to study.

White's insights about creativity in the Free Church tradition are intriguing because they indicate how a tradition that is known as "free" can have clear structure and background. Free Church does not mean "anything goes." White lists five opportunities for creativity within the worship service:[29] (1) Each congregation has the freedom to determine the order of the service. However, *how* the service is ordered constitutes a theological statement. (2) The sermon gives the clergy an opportunity to bring the themes of the service together in one focal event, (3) The pastoral prayers sum up the concerns of the congregation. In words that are similar to those of jazz musicians, White explains, "The supreme advantage of a good pastoral prayer is the opportunity to be creative in expressing the situation in time and space of a particular people. It can give voice to their unexpressed feelings with both authenticity and relevancy."[30] (4) The choice of the various propers provides other opportunities for creativity. (5) Finally, the musical and visual arts provide opportunities for creativity. He notes that these provide special expressions that are not the sole articulation of the clergy, but belong to the laity in particular. Structure provides freedom; freedom leads to greater participation by more people.

White's observations about freedom and creativity in the liturgy are similar to those we cited earlier about improvisation in jazz. Freedom within the liturgy does not warrant sloppiness, lack of constraint, or an attitude of "anything goes." Like jazz, the Free Church has adapted the relationship between freedom and constraint, solo and ensemble. Liturgy takes practice, just as the improvisational licks in a jazz solo. White explains, "One is free as long as one knows what is essential; without this knowledge one never dares stray too far from the sure and familiar. Liturgical knowledge, then, is a liberating discipline."[31] White explains that for creative worship to occur, education of both clergy and laity must take place. And finally, creative worship is service to the community done by the people of God. White notes:

> Nothing will be perceived as creative, no matter how original, without the clear sense that it is offered in loving service for others. After all, the worship is the congregation's own worship, not the clergy's masterpiece of creativity. One must know, accept, and love one's people for creativity to have any value in worship.[32]

The tradition of the Free Church offers an example of how tradition is adapted to the relevance of a particular congregation and its life. White's analysis indicates that even within those traditions we label as "free," certain constraints actually offer the fertile edge for worship. In fact, the interplay between freedom and structure, guided by the congregation's life story, creates a worship that is fresh and relevant. With sympathies similar to Luther's, White connects freedom with service to neighbor. Liturgy is the matrix for shaping people's lives for the task of reaching out to those in need.

Liturgy becomes a form of playing with the gospel. Freedom relies on tradition; tradition frees one to play. Kathleen Norris' stories of her times with monastic communities illustrate this point well. The ritual and rule of Saint Benedict provide the structure, much like the pattern of the twelve-bar blues, for the monks to find freedom. Norris remarks:

> The play in a monastery makes of life a continuous flow: church, refectory, workplace, church. Each place has its prayers and rituals, linking each activity as part of a whole. One feels

part of a story that is continually unfolding, being told and retold. Even the Benedictine motto, *orare est laborare*, insisting that work *is* prayer, is to my mind an essential playful attitude, one that may help account for the youthful countenances of so many monastics.[33]

Our quick-fix culture often has the notion that play is merely spontaneous and instantly gratifying. This consumerism can be seen in the kinds of toys that are marketed to children—instant success, instant gratification. As adults, we believe that in order to find time to play, we must step away from the routine. Yet on vacation, we find that the absence of routine can actually subvert our spontaneous play. The Benedictines, popularized in the writings of people such as Norris, may know something that the rest of us need to learn again. Familiar routines, shared in community, can actually bring life and delight.

In his wonderful exploration of jazz, *Thinking in Jazz: The Infinite Art of Improvisation,* Paul F. Berliner concludes the massive study with a chapter called "Jazz as a Way of Life." This chapter builds on the idea that jazz is a metaphor for living in this world. Berliner claims that "an unwavering commitment to learning and creativity characterizes the interrelated music specialties of jazz improvisers, and their passionate pursuits."[34] The metaphor of jazz as a way of life prepares us for living in an ambiguous world by interweaving the qualities of lifelong learning and disciplined creativity. Berliner comments on how jazz functions, in many ways that remind me of how the liturgy functions in Christian circles, to create a community of improvisers—by sharing the traditions that shape jazz and looking to the future of its traditions.

First, Berliner explains that jazz is a process of creativity that evolves over a lifetime. He uses analogies from literature and the visual arts. "An author once quipped that he never completes a novel so much as abandons it when it is sufficiently rewritten for him to begin another."[35] Jazz develops over time, and the performer/improviser is often discontent with the last performance, seeking to create new ways to work with the old. Like jazz musicians, we gather for worship in communal settings and we pray privately, but never for the sake of "getting it right." We return week after week to rehearse the dialogue, to say the same thing again in different ways. The power of the liturgy to shape communities is its resiliency over time, over many lifetimes. Good liturgy is as much the process of "never completing a novel" as it is the revision.

Berliner also compares learning jazz improvisation to learning a foreign language. Language acquisition comes through practice, listening to the various sounds, and immersion into the community of that language. "Participants in renowned foreign language programs agree to confine discourse exclusively to the language under study and then immerse themselves in their subject, its vocabulary, grammar and syntax, analyzing literature and practicing conversation during every social interaction."[36] Jazz musicians study the oral traditions of jazz, listen to recordings, go to clubs, play with others, practice idioms on their own. To be good at improvisation is to be good at the basics. Berliner works hard to dispel the "popular definitions of improvisation that emphasize only its spontaneous, intuitive nature" as "astonishingly incomplete."[37] How might our liturgical life change if we realized that to be good at "change," we must also be good at the basics, immersing ourselves in the language, stories, and symbols of tradition? It is not without coincidence that much of the best in feminist theology has been accomplished by those who also know tradition the best. Witness Elizabeth Johnson's marvelous work in *She Who Is: The Mystery of God in Feminist Theological Discourse.* Johnson's work would not be nearly as powerful without her powerful analysis of tradition.

Berliner similarly likens playing jazz to telling one's story, passing on the stories of others, and even feeling a part of a bigger, more cosmic and universal story. He explains that jazz musicians are required to put together bits and pieces of music to create musical stories that convey a beginning, middle, and end. The shapes of these stories are open for new possibilities. The playing of jazz is like the unfolding of a script on stage that is not yet finished. Novelty develops as patterns are explored in relationship to one another.[38] To express one's story in jazz is to be part of a larger, more cosmic narrative:

Finally, at the highest level are extraordinary transcendental experiences in which players feel, if only momentarily, "in touch with the big picture." Entering into another world of awareness and sensitivity, they feel a deep sense of reverence for "all living things." In spiritual communion, they merge together in the shine of a universal life force—timeless, peaceful, yet energizing and euphoric.[39]

In clear spiritual discourse, Berliner notes that the musical experience is a transcendent, spiritual experience. With language similar to that of a mystical experience, the performer is drawn into the "bigger picture." The individual is transcended, and the cosmic sense of life is felt and experienced. In other sections of the text, Berliner notes that these spiritual experiences are rooted in the past, "as if becoming joined to a long chain of expressive human history."[40] In language similar to that of Mihaly Csikszentmihalyi and Philip Hefner, Berliner talks about jazz as a way of life, of being in the world. One could call jazz a vocation. Improvisation is a source of life that participates in a larger, cosmic discourse. He even claims that jazz transcends cultural and historical boundaries, creating a universal experience.[41]

Where Might Improvisational Worship Lead?

Where might this model of improvisational worship lead? What might it look like? Here are some personal experiences that give pictures of what improvisational worship might be. These experiences also give a sense of the final direction and goal of improvisational worship: "to project an image that is intrinsically revolutionary...at radical odds with the status quo."[42]

Roman Catholics continually reflect on the radical changes that have occurred since Vatican II. An example of these radical changes is the architecture and worship style of the community of sisters at St. Benedict's in Saint Joseph, Minnesota. When I first entered their sanctuary, I knew immediately that something was different. Light streamed in through the windows above into the soft-hued sanctuary, which was supported by native marble and stone. Soft-curved lines wrapped around the altar, the focus of the chapel. The presider's chair was noticeably small and on the same level as the laity. Once an ornate Baroque chapel, this place reflected a new and different kind of Benedictine hospitality. Worship in this space enhances the deep spiritual lives of these women, for whom hospitality comes easily. Here, religious life intertwines with daily activities, marking as worship an ordinary event in extraordinary lives. Worship is not merely "receiving" the elements from the hierarchy, but actively welcoming others into the community as the people of God.

For many Roman Catholics, the sacraments are "rooted in the grace of daily life." As Bernard Cooke notes in the *National Catholic Reporter,* "When one speaks of the sacramental rituals 'giving grace,' one is talking about the transformation of people that takes place because of God's presence in the risen Christ and their Spirit."[43] What happens in liturgy is that we are transformed to love and serve the Lord. Liturgy is active; it propels us into the world. Cooke notes that though many Catholics may not be reflective about the changes in the liturgy, they are aware that "church" has changed. He comments:

> Hazy though the notion may still be for many, there is a common awareness that the church is the people of God, that all the baptized, and not just the ordained, share in mission and ministry and therefore in responsibility for the church and the world. This is beginning to move Catholics toward realizing that sacraments are not something they "receive"; rather, sacraments are actions they do, active professions of their faith. The Eucharist in particular is no longer unquestioningly viewed as "Father's thing."[44]

Because the ordinary stuff of our world is celebrated as a fit place for God's grace in the sacramental acts, the ordinary stuff of our lives prepares us for the liturgy. We are called by the liturgy to be transformed, to be alive in the world. How can we worship in our world so that we live in the world, yet see a vision bigger than our world? How can worship be both grounded in tradition and offer the imagination and inspiration of improvisation? The following categories lift up some elements of creative, life-giving, tradition-bearing, improvisational worship.

First, the church must be ecumenical, international, and cosmic in scope. In other words, we must broaden our vision beyond our own world to include the world of others and to include the creation of God. One resource for this vision is the sacramental vision of creation found in Roman Catholic theology. The sacramental vision extends God's grace to all the created order. The celebration of the sacraments is a cosmic celebration of God's infinite love. Our vision must also reach beyond our own boundaries and borders, to extend to those who are often considered "other" by many Christians. According to Cooke:

> Sacramental rituals must become celebrations of the Christian meaning of life as it is lived by a diversity of people in a diversity of cultures and a diversity of circumstances. We must be free to celebrate liturgies that "tell it as it is," liturgies that honor and preserve the traditions that helped us make us what we are, liturgies that heal us and animate us to be healers of today's world.[45]

The diverse, ambiguous world in which we live must be reflected in the liturgies we celebrate. Liturgy does not call us away from the world and its diversity, but deeply into the world. Jesus always warned those who valued ritual for its own sake. The celebration of the sacraments is a celebration of cosmic diversity.

Tradition is what we create through the improvisation of the tradition. On a recent trip to Wittenberg, Germany, for a conference sponsored by Lutheran World Federation, I had the experience of singing "Eine Feste Burg" with people from all around the world in Luther's own Schloskirke. Participants from LWF and local Germans joined together for a Reformation Day celebration. As we entered the sanctuary, we noted a large picture of Katharina von Bora, Luther's wife, with one of their children. The portrait was a segment from one of Lucas Cranach's famous Reformation paintings. The frame enclosed Katharina and her child in a way that resembled the Blessed Virgin Mary with the baby Jesus. Under the picture were the words: *Katharina von Bora, Die Reformer.* The entire service was devoted to lifting up the forgotten reformer. The service itself transformed and changed the traditional picture of the Reformation story. We learned about the strength, brilliance, character, and faith of Katharina. Too often she has been portrayed as only "Luther's wife." Both in the picture and in the service, Katharina was lifted up as a contrast between the strengths of this woman Reformer and the traditionally portrayed humble, meek qualities of the Virgin Mary. This service portrayed a strong woman who, in her own valuable ways, helped to change the nature of the church. These Germans caught in spirit what Patrick Henry says about history: "To say that history rhymes is to catch both the predictable and the unpredictable—the fundamental patterns that seem to repeat themselves but with manifold variations."[46] We live by the improvisation of the tradition into the revolution of the present.

It is time to remember with Luther that worship must be for all people. The church does not belong to the clergy. The Lutheran Confessions are adamant that the "chief purpose of all ceremonies is to teach the people what they need to know about Christ."[47] The adaptations from the Roman mass, propounded by the Reformers, seemed inconspicuous at first: German hymns were sung; scripture was available in the vernacular; the bread *and* wine were offered to the laity. Yet what appeared to be insignificant changes challenged the heart of the church's hierarchy. Melanchthon is famous for saying "To know Christ is to know his benefits." Yet clearly, the benefits had not been available to all. Luther and the Reformers challenged the power structures at the very root of the church—in the experience of worship. Their liturgical reforms challenged "what they need to know about Christ." The Reformation connected the benefits of Christ to the faith of each believer. Liturgy is the most powerful when it re-forms the life of each individual person. What might look different if we were to reinterpret the priesthood of all believers for our time and setting?

Worship leads to transformation. In his usual style, Luther begins the Large Catechism with a preface that urges his fellow Germans to study it carefully. Buried deep within Luther's passionate words is the sense that learning its contents will change one's life. Luther was aware of the upheavals that were happening in society; the way the world was had changed forever. The very thing he believed in was what threatened to turn the Christian world into hundreds of factions. Luther urges Christians, especially pastors, to study and read:

> Let all Christians exercise themselves in the Catechism daily,
> and constantly put it into practice, guarding themselves with
> the greatest care and diligence against the poisonous infection
> of such security or vanity. Let them continue to read and
> teach, to learn and meditate and ponder. Let them never stop
> until they have proved by experience that they have taught
> the devil to death and have become wiser than God himself
> and all his saints.[48]

Diligence in study, like the fruits of the Spirit, lead one to deeper
faith. Luther wrote several hymns based on sections of the
catechism, and he also preached from the catechism. The constant
reading and teaching among the laity changed the way that
Christian theology and worship would be done. No longer was
it simply in the hands of a few elite clergy or religious orders.
Faith is for everyone; God's grace is not selective. The formation
of tradition in our lives should lead us to revolutionary acts in
service to the neighbor. However, I realize, along with many
others, that my own catechismal training led to the opposite.

Worship is grounded in Word and sacrament. The sacraments
and the proclamation of the Word offer the roots of Christianity,
which can free the believer to challenge the bondage of the
present moments. Like Luther's use of baptism to form the
priesthood of all believers, feminist theologians have challenged
the exclusivity of a male priesthood. Torvend explains, "At its
heart, the church is a Eucharistic community...As Eucharistic
food and drink are given to all in equal proportion and without
discrimination, so those who receive this food and drink pledge
themselves to the care of the world's hungry."[49] Or in the words
of the traditional documents, "the chief purpose of all ceremonies
is to teach the people what they need to know about Christ."[50]
The symbols of baptism and eucharist are free gifts to all God's
people, challenging the discriminatory lifestyles of those of us
who exclude the rest of the world through our materialism,
racism, and sexism.

How can the church be a radical witness to a broken world
when its own centers are so fragmented and broken? We often
use "the ceremonies of worship" as a means by which we destroy

any hope of community and unity in the Spirit. Diversity of expression is needed; uniformity of expression is not desirable. As churches struggle with questions of unity and diversity, I find that my tradition's own confessional writings can be a good historical conversation partner. Though we are not tied to them in a legalistic way, they can remain as living conversation partners to remind us that the struggles we face today have historical roots. We must find our unity not in ceremonies, liturgies, or doctrines, but in the freedom of the gospel to serve the neighbor. The point of the "service" is precisely that—to go in peace and *serve* the Lord. Doxology follows. Christianity is finally a way of life.

For Lutherans, the Augsburg Confession grounds the articles of faith and doctrine in the chief articles of God, original sin, and the Son of God. Even the article concerning justification, the article for Luther by which the church stands or falls, *follows* the three ecumenical articles. This understanding must be preserved when trying to reflect on the role of worship and ecclesiology. For Melanchthon, the defining characteristics of church are Word and sacrament. These two provide an ecumenical understanding of church and of worship. Melanchthon defines church in Article Seven:

> The assembly of all believers among whom the Gospel is preached in its purity and the holy sacraments are administered according to the Gospel. For it is sufficient for the true unity of the Christian church that the Gospel be preached in conformity with a pure understanding of it and that the sacraments be administered in accordance with the divine Word. It is not necessary for the true unity of the Christian church that ceremonies, instituted by men, should be observed uniformly in all places. It is as Paul says in Eph. 4:4–5: "There is one body and one Spirit, just as you were called to the one hope that belongs to your call, one Lord, one faith, one baptism."[51]

Melanchthon's understanding of the role of ritual in church is similar to that of Luther's emphasis that the reign of God is not bound in rituals or rites, but found through faith in the Holy

Spirit. Unity in the church has less to do with ritual and worship and more to do with life in the Spirit. The Holy Spirit enlivens, quickens, and energizes the community of saints, the *ecclesia tou theou*. This historical example from my own Lutheran tradition is ironic, however, in light of the worship wars that threaten to fracture and break apart the church. The Lutheran Confessions warning, written 450 years ago, seems even more appropriate today.

Finally, worship focuses the ethical goal of the Christian life. The goal of the worship is to equip Christians to serve the neighbor, that is, the whole creation. When we leave the sanctuary on Sunday morning, many of our liturgies end with the presiding minister's saying, "Go in peace to love and serve the Lord." "Thanks be to God!" we all reply in unison. This is the point of Christian worship. How many times I have said that and given very little thought to the power of those words. I found in the writings of Albert Murray the appropriate connection between the ethical dimension of writing and composing when he says:

> Indeed, the most valid aspiration as well as the most urgent necessity for any writer who truly takes the social, which is to say, the ethical, function of fiction seriously is not to create something at least different if not new, but rather to achieve something natural to himself and to his sense of life, namely a stylization adequate to the complexity of the experience of his time and place—perhaps with the lack of past masters, something that is more than merely adequate.[52]

The point, of course, is to take the social and ethical function of worship together. The power of his words is that the ethical function of worship is not necessarily to create something completely new but to achieve "something natural to himself and to his sense of life." The ethical function of worship is contextual in a local and universal sense. "Go in peace to love and serve the Lord" is about finding our service in our own context, but also within the larger social and communal arena. The service is rooted in the mission of the local community and congregation in our own time and place.

Some Thoughts for the Next Generation

I don't know what to say to my goddaughter about her future in the church. She was baptized in the Lutheran church and is being raised by a Roman Catholic mother and a Methodist father. What worries me are the long conversations I've had with Janet, her mother, about how to raise Abbie in a Christian environment that doesn't continue the patriarchal abuses her mother experienced growing up in a strict Roman Catholic environment. I would like to say my own tradition is different, but I know better. While Lutherans may ordain women, we still exclude gays and lesbians from the ordained ministry; we have rarely changed the exclusive language in our services; and we often worry about the numbers instead of the mission. I'm part of the problem as well. I don't know that leaving the church is an answer for Janet, Ross, and Abbie. But staying in the church as it remains is not an option either. What can I tell Abbie Josephine? What will her future in the church be?

Abbie's dilemma is finally my own dilemma. I belong to a church whose radical message of freedom in the gospel has wedded itself to the market-driven culture of American materialism. Luther's words sound a contemporary warning:

> The faith of this sacrament has become utterly extinct, and the holy sacrament has been turned into mere merchandise, a market, and a profit-making business. Hence participations, brotherhoods, intercessions, merits, anniversaries, memorial days and the like wares are bought and sold, traded and bartered, in the church. On these the priests and monks depend for their entire livelihood.[53]

We worry if we don't grow enough; we send people to be trained at Disney World. Worship turns Mickey Mouse, and the images of other Dachaus haunt our national news at every moment. Where must the church turn? Once again, tradition might offer the most revolutionary images. Jesus' own words show us how the church might find its heart again: "The Spirit of the Lord is upon me, because he has anointed me to bring good news to the poor. He has sent me to proclaim release to the captives and recovery of sight to the blind, to let the oppressed go free, to proclaim the year of the Lord's favor" (Lk. 4:18–19). To listen to the poor, to see with the eyes of the blind, to hear with the deaf will find favor with the Lord. The roots of the gospel are in service to the neighbor. So maybe I can help Abbie find those voices that will help us all to listen to new tunes, to new ways of translating the tradition into the vernacular, creating a revolutionary image of hope for the world.

> *THE DOCTRINE of creation is the beginning point for the story of God's creative and redeeming work in the world. The church's mission is to improvise on that theme anew in each generation.*

NOTES

Preface

[1]James Baldwin, "Sonny's Blues," Anthology of American Literature, vol. 2, edited by George McMichael (New York: Macmillan Publishing Co., Inc., 1974), 1798.

Chapter 1

[1]Mary Catherine Bateson, *Composing a Life* (New York: Plume/Penguin Books, 1989), 2–3, 17–18.

[2]Patrick Henry, *The Ironic Christian's Companion: Finding the Marks of God's Grace in the World* (New York: Riverhead Books, 1999).

[3]Ibid., 5, 8.

[4]Gen. 1:1–2 "In the beginning when God created the heavens and the earth, the earth was a formless void and darkness covered the face of the deep, while a wind from God swept over the face of the waters." Gen. 2:4b–7: "In the day that the LORD God made the earth and the heavens, when no plant of the field was yet in the earth and no herb of the field had yet sprung up—for the LORD God had not caused it to rain upon the earth, and there was no one to till the ground; but a stream would rise from the earth, and water the whole face of the ground—then the LORD God formed man from the dust of the ground, and breathed into his nostrils the breath of life; and the man became a living being." Ps. 8:3–8: "When I look at your heavens, the work of your fingers, the moon and the stars that you have established; what are human beings that you are mindful of them, mortals that you care for them? Yet you have made them a little lower than God, and crowned them with glory and honor. You have given them dominion over the works of your hands; you have put all things under their feet, all sheep and oxen, and also the beasts of the field, the birds of the air, and the fish of the sea, whatever passes along the paths of the seas." Jn. 1:1–5: "In the beginning was the Word, and the Word was with God, and the Word was God. He was in the beginning with God. All things came into being through him, and without him not one thing came into being. What has come into being in him was life, and the life was the light of all people. The light shines in the darkness, and the darkness did not overcome it." Col. 1:15–20: "He is the image of the invisible God, the firstborn of all creation; for in him all things in heaven and on earth were created, things visible and invisible, whether thrones or dominions or rulers or powers—all things have been created through him and for him. He himself is before all things, and in him all things hold together. He is the head of the body, the church; he is the beginning, the firstborn from the dead, so that he might come to have first place in everything. For in him all the fullness of God was pleased to dwell, and through him God was pleased to reconcile to himself all things, whether on earth or in heaven, by making peace through the blood of his cross."

[5]Alfred North Whitehead, *Religion in the Making* (New York: Fordham University Press, 1996), 147.

[6]Gustaf Wingren, "The Doctrine of Creation: Not an Appendix but the First Article," *Word and World* 4, no. 4 (Fall, 1984): 353.

[7]Ibid., 361.

[8]Ibid., 357.

[9]Ibid., 360.

[10]Philip Hefner, *The Human Factor* (Minneapolis: Fortress Press, 1993), 253.

[11]Philip Sheldrake, *Living Between Worlds: Place and Journey in Celtic Spirituality* (London: Darton-Langman-Todd, 1995), 71.

[12]Saint Patrick's Breastplate, "I Bind Unto Myself Today," in *Lutheran Book of Worship* (Minneapolis: Augsburg Publishing House; Philadelphia: Board of Publication, Lutheran Church in America, 1978), no. 188.

[13]Philip Newell, *Listening for the Heartbeat of God: A Celtic Spirituality* (London: SPCK, 1997), 13.

[14]Elizabeth Johnson, *She Who Is: The Mystery of God in Feminist Theological Discourse* (New York: Crossroad, 1993), 133–34.

[15]Ibid., 214.

[16]Susan Ross, *Extravagant Affections: A Feminist Sacramental Theology* (New York: Continuum, 1998), 35.

[17]Ted Peters, ed., *Cosmos as Creation: Theology and Science in Consonance* (Nashville: Abingdon Press, 1989), 45–65.

[18]Ross, 205.

[19]Ibid., 208.

[20]For the development of these three models, I am drawing on the work of Ian Barbour, Sallie McFague, and Philip Hefner.

[21]Ian Barbour, *Religion and Science: Historical and Contemporary Issues* (San Francisco: Harper San Francisco, 1997), 3.

[22]Ibid., 281.

[23]Ibid., 6.

[24]John Gillespie, *The Musical Experience* (Belmont, Calif.: Wadsworth, 1972), 84.

[25]Barbour, 81.

[26]Ibid., 306.

[27]Ibid., chapter 1.

[28]Ibid., 88.

[29]Ibid., 9.

[30]Gillespie, 115.

[31]Ibid., 119.

[32]Robert Burns, *Epistle to Robert Graham, Esq, of Fintry: Requesting a Favour,* quoted in Gillespie, 161.

[33]Gillespie, 180.

[34]Ibid., 214.

[35]Ibid.

[36]Barbour, 281–84.

[37]Anton Webern, *The Path to New Music,* quoted in Gillespie, 337.

[38]Philip Hefner, "The Evolution of the Created Co-Creator," in *An Evolving Dialogue: Scientific, Historical, Philosophical and Theological Perspectives on Evolution,* ed. James B. Miller (Washington, D.C.: American Association for the Advancement of Science, 1998), 418.

[39]Douglas John Hall, *God and Human Suffering* (Minneapolis: Augsburg, 1986), 74.

[40]Ibid., 81.

[41]Gillespie, 483.

[42]Ibid., 484.x

[43]Ibid.

[44]Max Roach quote from *Thinking in Jazz: The Infinite Art of Improvisation,* by Paul F. Berliner (Chicago and London: University of Chicago Press, 1994), 417.

[45]Stephen Richter, "The Beauty of Building, Dwelling and Monk: Aesthetics, Religion, and the Architectural Qualities of Jazz," *African American Review* 29, no. 2 (Summer 1995): 259.

[46]Peters, *Cosmos as Creation.*

[47]Richter, "The Beauty of Building," 4.

[48]Hefner, *The Human Factor.*

[49]John Haught, "Does Evolution Rule Out God's Existence?" in Miller, 348.

[50]Ibid., 349–50.

[51]Elizabeth Johnson, "Does God Play Dice? Divine Providence and Chance," in Miller, 368.

Chapter 2

[1]Bateson, 240.

[2]Dorothee Soelle, *To Work and To Love: A Theology of Creation* (Philadelphia: Fortress Press, 1984), 43.

[3]Hefner, *The Human Factor,* 20.

[4]Mary Catherine Bateson, *Peripheral Visions: Learning Along the Way* (New York: HarperCollins, 1994), 9.

[5]Bateson, *Composing a Life,* 3.

[6]Ibid., 2.

[7]Bateson, *Peripheral Visions,* 11.

[8] Ibid., 10.

[9]Ibid., 194.

[10]Alfonso Montuori, "Social Creativity, Academic Discourse, and the Improvisation of Inquiry," *Revision* 20, no. 1 (Summer 1997): 34.

[11]Ibid., 4.

[12]Ibid., 5.

[13]Flow: "a state of consciousness in which concentration on activity is so intense that completed absorption is achieved," in "How to Find Flow," interview with Mihaly Csikszentmihalyi, *Free Inquiry* 18, no. 3 (Summer 1998): 25

[14]Csikszentmihalyi, *Creativity: Flow and the Psychology of Discovery and Invention* (New York: HarperCollins, 1996), 23.

[15]Paul F. Berliner, *Thinking in Jazz: The Infinite Art of Improvisation* (Chicago and London: University of Chicago Press, 1994), 486.

[16]Martin H. Levinson, "Mapping Creativity with a Capital 'C,'" *ETC: A Review of General Semantics* 54, no. 4 (Winter 1997): 447.

[17]Csikszentmihalyi, *Creativity,* 27.

[18]Ibid., 41.

[19]Ibid., 42.

[20]Ibid., 31.

[21]Red Rodney, quoted in Berliner, 485.

[22]Ibid., 51.

[23]"1. Creative individuals have a great deal of physical energy, but they are also often quiet and at rest. 2. Creative individuals tend to be smart, yet also naive at the same time. 3. A third paradoxical trait refers to the related combination of playfulness and discipline, or responsibility and irresponsibility. 4. Creative individuals alternate between imagination and fantasy at one end, and a rooted sense of reality at the other. 5. Creative people seem to harbor opposite tendencies on the continuum between extroversion and introversion. 6. Creative individuals are also remarkably humble and proud at the same time. 7. In all cultures, men are brought up to be 'masculine' and to disregard and repress those aspects of their temperament that the culture regards as 'feminine,' whereas women are expected to do the opposite. Creative individuals to a certain extent escape this rigid gender role stereotyping. 8. Generally creative people are thought to be rebellious and independent. 9. Most creative persons are very *passionate* about their work, yet they can be extremely *objective* about it as well. 10. Finally, the openness and sensitivity of creative individuals often exposes them to *suffering and pain yet also a great deal of enjoyment.*" Csikszentmihalyi, *Creativity,* 58–73.

[24]Ibid., 111.

[25]Flow has nine main elements: "1. There are clear goals every step of the way. 2. There is immediate feedback to one's actions. 3. There is balance between challenges and skills. 4. Action and awareness are merged. 5. Distractions are excluded from consciousness. 6. There is no worry of failure. 7. Self-consciousness disappears. 8. The sense of time becomes distorted. 9. The activity becomes autotelic." Ibid., 111–13.

[26]Alfred North Whitehead, *Process and Reality: An Essay in Cosmology* (New York: Free Press, 1978), 5.

[27]Csikszentmihalyi, *Creativity*, 5.

[28]"Mihaly Csikszentmihalyi," *Omni* 17, no. 4 (January 1995): 73.

[29]Ibid., 9.

[30]Soelle, 39.

[31]Whitehead, *Process and Reality*, 348. "God and the World are the contrasted opposites in terms of which Creativity achieves its supreme task of transforming disjoined multiplicity, with its diversities in opposition, into concrescent unity, with its diversities in contrast."

[32] Alfred North Whitehead, *Essays in Science and Philosophy* (New York: Philosophical Library, 1947), 15.

[33]Whitehead, *Process and Reality*, 346.

[34]Whitehead, *Science and Philosophy*, 15.

[35]Soelle, 48, 49.

[36]Berliner, 498.

[37]John B. Cobb, Jr., *Christ in a Pluralistic Age* (Philadelphia: Westminster Press, 1975), 43.

[38]Ibid., 21.

[39]Berliner, 491.

[40]Ibid., 492.

[41]John B. Cobb, Jr., "Christ Beyond Creative Transformation," in *Encountering Jesus*, ed. Stephen T. Davis (Atlanta: John Knox Press, 1988), 142–43.

[42]Ibid., 143 (italics are in the original).

[43]Ibid., 141.

[44]John B. Cobb, Jr., "Postmodern Christianity in Quest of Eco-Justice," 3, (public lecture in Chicago, February 1990).

[45]John B. Cobb, Jr., "The Presence of the Past and the Eucharist," *Process Studies* 13 (Fall 1983): 218.

[46]Janna Tull Steed, *Duke Ellington: A Spiritual Biography* (New York: Crossroad, 1999), 164.

[47]Cobb, *Christ in a Pluralistic Age*, 228.

[48]Ibid., 185.

[49]Ibid., 186.

[50]Ibid., 187.

[51]Ibid., 182.

[52]Ibid., 183.

[53]Ibid.

[54]Ibid.

[55]Alfred North Whitehead, *Adventures in Ideas* (New York: Free Press, Macmillan, 1961), 296.

[56]Ibid., 286.

[57]Berliner, 503.

[58]Hefner, *The Human Factor*, 35.

[59]Ibid., 17.

[60]Ibid., 49.

[61]Ibid., 55–56.

[62]Ibid., 19.

[63]Ibid., 29.

[64]Hefner, "The Evolution of the Created Co-Creator," 417.

[65]Hefner, *The Human Factor*, 154.

[66]Hefner, "The Evolution of the Created Co-Creator," 418.

[67]Elizabeth Johnson, *Women, Earth, and Creator Spirit* (New York/Mahwah: Paulist Press, 1993), 58.

[68]Ibid., 43–44.

[69]Ibid., 44.

[70]Hefner, *The Human Factor*, 42–43.

[71]Ibid., 44.

[72]Bateson, *Composing a Life*, 234.

Chapter 3

[1]Max De Pree, *Leadership Jazz* (New York: Dell Publishing, 1992), 8–9.

[2]Bateson, *Peripheral Visions,* 233.

[3]Ibid., 93.

[4]Ibid., 62.

[5]Arthur Peacocke, *Theology for a Scientific Age* (London: Basil Blackwell, 1990), 173.

[6]Ibid., 175.

[7]Ibid.

[8]M. Mitchell Waldrop, *Complexity: The Emerging Science at the Edge of Order and Chaos* (New York: Touchstone Books, Simon & Schuster, 1992), 17.

[9]Ibid., 30.

[10]Berliner, chapter 2.

[11]Ibid., 41.

[12]Ibid., 59.

[13]DePree, 9.

[14]Daniel Belgrad, *The Culture of Spontaneity: Improvisation and the Arts in Postwar America* (Chicago: University of Chicago Press, 1998), 179–80.

[15]Ibid., 184–85.

[16]Sallie McFague, *Models of God: Theology for an Ecological, Nuclear Age* (Philadelphia: Fortress Press, 1987), xii.

[17]Ibid.

[18]Ibid., xiii.

[19]Joseph Sittler, *The Structure of Christian Ethics* (Baton Rouge, La.: Louisiana State University Press, 1958), 7.

[20]Ian Barbour, *Religion in an Age of Science* (San Francisco: Harper San Francisco, 1990), 269.

[21]Paul Sponheim, *Faith and the Other* (Minneapolis: Fortress Press, 1993), chapter 4.

[22]Barbour, *Religion in an Age of Science*, 269.

[23]Ibid.

[24]Sittler, 50.

[25]Joseph Bracken, "Response to Elizabeth Johnson's 'Does God Play Dice?'" *Theological Studies* 57, no. 4 (December 1996): 6.

[26]Bateson, *Composing a Life,* 3.

[27]Sittler, 66.

[28]Larry Rasmussen, "Shaping Communities," in *Practicing Our Faith: A Way of Life for a Searching People,* ed. Dorothy C. Bass (San Francisco: Jossey-Bass, 1997), 121.

[29]Ibid., 125.

[30]Ibid.

[31]Ibid.

[32]Ibid., 129.

[33]Ibid., 132.

[34]John B. Cobb, Jr., *Lay Theology* (St. Louis: Chalice Press, 1994), 101.

[35]Philip Hefner, "The Demographics of Possibility: People's Church," *Currents in Theology and Mission* 24, no. 4 (August 1998): 294.

[36]Ibid., 312.

[37]Philip Hefner, "The Church as Well of Possibility," *Currents in Theology and Mission* 25, no. 4 (August 1998): 261.

[38]Eric W. Gritsch and Robert W. Jenson, *Lutheranism: The Theological Movement and Its Confessional Writings* (Philadelphia: Fortress Press, 1976), 125.

[39]Ibid., 124–25.

[40]Ibid., 126.

[41]Ibid.

[42]Ibid., 131.

[43]Ibid.

[44]Cobb, *Lay Theology,* 86.

[45]Ibid., 87.

[46]Ibid., 91.

[47]Dietrich Bonhoeffer, *Life Together,* trans. John W. Doberstein (San Francisco: Harper & Row, 1954), 25.

[48]Berliner, 36.

Chapter 4

[1]Albert Murray, "The Omni-American: Interview with Albert Murray," interview by Tony Scherman, *American Heritage* 47, no. 5 (September 1996).

[2]David Whiteis, "Blues on the Move: Jumpin' the Blues," *Down Beat* 61, no. 7 (July 1994).

[3]"Glory Be to Jesus," *Lutheran Book of Worship,* no. 95.

[4]Darby Kathleen Ray, *Deceiving the Devil: Atonement, Abuse, and Ransom* (Cleveland: Pilgrim Press, 1998), vii.

[5]Ibid.

[6]Robert McAfee Brown, *Theology in a New Key: Responding to Liberation Themes* (Philadelphia: Westminster Press, 1978), 12. I want to thank Douglas Oakman for introducing me to this text. This book has been immensely helpful for connections in my work. Brown's main source for his book was the liberation theologies of Latin America.

[7]Ibid., 25.

[8]Ibid., 27.

[9]Baldwin, 1799–1800.

[10]James H. Cone, *The Spirituals and the Blues* (Maryknoll: Orbis Books, 1972, 1991), 105.

[11]Ibid., 103.

[12]Baldwin, 1775.

[13]Ibid., 1779.

[14]Ibid., 1797.

[15]Ibid., 1798.

[16]Ibid.

[17]Ibid., 1997.

[18]"And the drugs which plagued Sonny still ravish his daughters and sons, and jazz persists, goes on…Creole would say that it's still getting in the water that matters. It doesn't matter when the song is played, or how long, but by whom. The jazz is never really over, it stays in the twisted face of the horn players even after the solo, in the desperate grip of the bass player when his moment on the big fiddle is over. Finding better times, making them, is enough. It doesn't matter where you travel, where you visit. And at the end, like jazz, getting there is finally the most important." "Letters from the Thirties." *The North American Review* 282, no. 3–4 (May-August 1997): 7.

[19]Baldwin, 1800.

[20]Tracey Sherard, "Sonny's Bebop: Baldwin's 'Blues Text' as Intracultural Critique," *African American Review* 32, no. 4 (1998): 691.

[21]Ibid., 693.

[22]Ibid., 704.

[23]Cone, 98.

[24]Ibid., 100.

[25]Stephen T. Asthma, "The Blues Artist as Cultural Rebel," *Humanist* 57, no. 4 (July-August 1997): 2.

[26]Ibid., 2.

[27]Angela Y. Davis, *Blues Legacies and Black Feminism: Gertrude "Ma" Rainey, Bessie Smith, and Billie Holiday* (New York: Vintage Books/Random House, 1999), 7.

[28]Ibid., 7.

[29]Ibid., 8.

[30]Ibid.

31Ibid., 9.
32Ibid., 41.
33Albert Murray, *The Hero and the Blues* (New York: Vintage Books, 1996), 83.
34Ibid., 82.
35Ibid., 83.
36Ibid., 84.
37Ibid., 85.
38Ibid., 86.
39Ibid., 88.
40Ibid., 107.
41Cone, 112.
42Ibid., 98.
43Ibid.
44Ibid., 99.
45Asthma, 3.
46Ibid., 4.
47Cone, 121.
48Ray, vii.
49Ibid., 122–23.
50Ibid., 128.
51Ibid., 132.
52Ibid., 139.
53Ibid., 144.
54Cone, 106.
55Ibid., 103.
56Ibid., 106.
57Murray, 101.

Chapter 5

1Quoted with permission from a personal letter from Vernon C. Holmquist to his niece Ann Pederson.
2Ross, 10.
3Annie Dillard, *For the Time Being* (New York: Alfred A. Knopf, 1999), 85.
4Marva Dawn, *Reaching Out without Dumbing Down: A Theology of Worship for the Turn-of-the-Century Culture* (Grand Rapids, Mich.: Eerdmans, 1995), 145.
5Ibid., 133.
6Annie Dillard, quoted in the foreword by Martin Marty in Dawn, ix.
7Samuel Torvend, "How Does the Liturgy Serve the Life of the World?" in *What Are the Ethical Implications of Worship?* by Steven Larson, H. Paul Santmire, and Samuel Torvend. From *Open Questions in Worship,* ed. Gordon Lathrop (Minneapolis: Fortress Press, 1996), 25.
8Ibid., 27.
9Ibid.
10Martin Luther, "The Babylonian Captivity of the Church," trans. A. T. W. Steinhauser, and revised by Frederick C. Ahrens and Abdel Ross Wentz, in *Three Treatises* (Philadelphia: Fortress Press, 1970), 152.
11 Torvend, 34.
12Dawn, 130.
13Joseph Sittler, *Gravity and Grace*, ed. Linda-Marie Delloff (Minneapolis: Augsburg, 1986), 94–95.
14Dawn, 141.
15Murray, 71.
16Ibid., 66.
17Ibid., 71.
18Ibid., 72.

[19]Ibid., 80, 81.

[20]Martin Luther, "Freedom of a Christian," trans. W. A. Lambert, revised by Jarold J. Grimm, in *Three Treatises* (Philadelphia: Fortress Press, 1970), 284–85.

[21]Martin Luther, "To the Christian Nobility of the German Nation," trans. Charles M. Jacobs, revised by James Atkinson, in *Three Treatises*, 10–11.

[22]Ibid., 12.

[23]Ibid., 24.

[24]Luther, "The Babylonian Captivity of the Church," in *Three Treatises*, 137.

[25]Luther, "To the Christian Nobility of the German Nation," in *Three Treatises*, 63.

[26]Martin Luther, *Luther's Works*, ed. Ulrich S. Leupold, vol. 53 (Philadelphia: Fortress Press, 1965), 19.

[27]James White, "Creativity: The Free Church Tradition," in *Liturgy: A Creative Tradition*, ed. Mary Collins and David Power, English language editor, Marcus Lefebure (Edinburgh and New York: T&T Clark and Seabury Press, 1983), 47–49.

[28]Ibid., 48.

[29]Ibid., 48–51.

[30]Ibid., 50.

[31]Ibid., 51.

[32]Ibid., 52.

[33]Kathleen Norris, *Dakota: A Spiritual Geography* (New York: Ticknor & Fields, 1993), 212.

[34]Berliner, 485.

[35]Ibid., 486.

[36]Ibid., 492.

[37]Ibid.

[38]Ibid., 493.

[39]Ibid., 498.

[40]Ibid., 491.

[41]Ibid.

[42]Murray, 80, 81.

[43]Bernard Cooke, "Sacraments Rooted in Grace of Daily Life," *National Catholic Reporter* 32, no.11 (10 November 1995), 2.

[44]Ibid.

[45]Ibid.

[46]Henry, 43.

[47]Theodore G. Tappert, ed. and trans., *The Book of Concord: The Confessions of the Evangelical Lutheran Church* (Philadelphia: Muhlenberg Press, 1959), 56.

[48]Ibid., 361.

[49]Torvend, 32.

[50]Tappert, 56.

[51]Ibid., 32.

[52]Murray, 81.

[53]Luther, "The Babylonian Captivity of the Church," *in Three Treatises*, 152.